Diamonds in the Garbage

By Sara C. Forsberg

Dedication

I would like to thank my family, friends, and all the people God brought into my life for their prayerful support and encouraging words that helped make my dream a reality. I would like to add a special thank you to Heather Johnson, my editor, for her encouragement, moral support, and expertise.

When Jesus spoke again to the people, he said, "I am the light of the world. Whoever follows me will never walk in darkness, but will have the light of life." (John 8:12)

Table of Contents

Introduction

"For I know the plans I have for you," declares the LORD, *"plans to prosper you and not to harm you, plans to give you hope and a future."* (Jeremiah 29:11 NIV)

A skeptic might ask, "Can it be true? Would God speak through a piece of jewelry?" The answer is *Yes!* My imagination is active, but this story is about more than my own self-talk. One conversation with my Lord changed the focus of my life.

One beautiful Minnesota summer morning, I was weeding our newly planted flowers. As I reached out to grab a piece of quack grass, I realized my new diamond tennis bracelet was missing.

The bracelet had been a spur-of-the-moment purchase during a vacation with my husband, Frank. In the Caribbean Islands there are jewelry stores on every street corner. We wandered into a small, quaint shop where I discovered the bracelet. It was a beauty. I loved its simplicity and sparkle, and quickly decided it should come home with me. After a little of my coaxing, or should I say whining, my husband agreed. After we returned home, I had the bracelet appraised for insurance purposes and its value was listed at three times what we had paid! I am notorious for misplacing, losing, or breaking jewelry my husband has given me in the past, so I wanted to make sure to keep this gift safe. I even had the clasp redone to lessen the chance that I might lose it.

As I looked down at my empty wrist that morning, I thought, "Okay, it's gone. I've lost it! How am I going to explain this?" I silently prayed, "God, you know where my bracelet is, and although you have a lot of important stuff going on, could you help me out here?"

I decided to retrace my steps. It was around one o'clock in the afternoon and during the day I had been in various parts of our home doing the things that moms and wives do to restore order. Following my path in reverse was a challenge. My search began where I was, in the garden. I made my way back to the house, hunting in the grass as I walked. I repeated the process in the kitchen, our bedroom and bathroom, and the shower. Again I muttered a little halfhearted prayer and bargained with God, "If you help me here, I promise to try harder to be a better person."

While I searched, I devised a way to disguise the loss from my husband, but I knew he would eventually learn the truth. He would shake his head sadly and I would be consigned forever to a life with only costume jewelry.

I sensed encouragement to check the garbage. I argued silently, "No, I am not going to check the stinky garbage." I continued to try to retrace my morning route. After searching a while longer, the idea to check the garbage returned, only this time, it seemed more like a gentle command.

I stubbornly thought, "No, I will not walk up there and I will not check the garbage. That is just plain stupid!" But the suggestion persisted. I said out loud, somewhat exasperated because I knew there would be no bracelet in the garbage can, "Okay, but I don't know why I am doing this."

I walked slowly and dejectedly through our garage and down our driveway to the dirty black canister. I was going to prove that there was no jewelry in that bin! It was ridiculous to imagine my lovely bracelet anywhere close to the garbage can—especially because I was certain I did not take the trash out that morning.

I opened the cover, revealing several plastic bags full of rubbish, and lifted out one bag at a time until they were positioned all around me on the ground. I tipped the empty container and just then I caught a glimpse of something rope-like and about the size of a rubber band at the bottom. Could it be my bracelet? I tilted the canister further and stuck my head into the can. It *was* my precious bracelet at the bottom! My beautiful diamond bracelet was in the trashcan, surrounded by paper wrappers and coffee grounds. At that moment, I heard the clear and compelling message, "I want you to write a book titled *Diamonds in the Garbage*."

"Me? Write a book? And what would this book be about?"

"*Diamonds in the Garbage* will be a love story. My work on Earth is done through people and you need to write to the women whom I place in your life. I transform the ordinary into the extraordinary. I bring healing to the wounded and love, joy, and peace are the fruits of a life focused on me."

It was the first time I heard an audible voice in my spirit. It wasn't a random thought; it was a clear instruction to do something that had never crossed my mind. At first I dismissed the directive as being a fluke, but I could not fully reject the inexplicable message. However, I did nothing to pursue writing except to continue making entries in my journal.

Several years passed and my mother was moved into a care facility near our home. There, I met a wonderful woman who played music, taught simple crafts, and encouraged the residents with activities. We found common interests and began to meet for occasional lunch dates. Eventually we both shared our desire to write. She shared her aspiration to write about her husband's unique childhood and I told her about my diamonds in the garbage. We made the decision to attend classes together and for two years we honed our writing skills at a community college. Our little group expanded to include another woman and we three bonded over the love of writing.

Although I received encouragement from friends, family, and our instructor, three more years passed and the book (except for the introduction which I wrote for a class assignment) was nonexistent. As I sat by my ailing mother's bedside, I whispered a promise to her that I would return to writing. I would write *Diamonds in the Garbage*. Buoyed by this promise, I once again had great intentions to initiate the business of writing, but still—no book! More years passed and I hadn't budged beyond writing the introduction. Over that time, my faith was strengthened and challenged, and my life was complicated by worry and loss, all of which created bountiful inspiration and stories to be told, but still—no book!

Recently, I began to search for the connection between a diamond bracelet lost in the garbage and my own life. Why had this event been so profound? I examined what had happened that day: I opened the lid and confronted the garbage inside. I actually surrounded myself in junk because it was my last resort, the only way I could find my lost treasure. Once that was accomplished I could move forward.

It occurred to me that my pretty bracelet is the perfect metaphor for my life and the lives of many other women. I know there are women just like my diamond bracelet, who have become lost in cavernous garbage cans, buried in trash. Some of the trash might be unfulfilled dreams, unrealistic expectations, emotional wounding, or unhealthy thinking and addictive behaviors. Their brilliance is hidden. Unfortunately, there is not always someone willing to dive into that garbage to find them. Sometimes, you have to seek help.

God's desire is for us to see ourselves as He sees us: precious and irreplaceable gems. He wants us to realize we are whole and healthy women who can be fully released from our rubbish and completely restored. God longs for us to know Him so intimately that we shine with the love made possible through a relationship with Jesus Christ. I invite you to share my story of putting aside the trash and emerging with the beautiful sparkle of a diamond.

The LORD is close to the brokenhearted and saves those who are crushed in spirit. (Psalms 34:18)

Amen!

Action plan

1. To begin the process of recovering your radiance, building your strengths, and releasing your talents, obtain a notebook and a pen to keep in a special place for daily writing.

Hues of You

Then he told them what they could expect for themselves: "Anyone who intends to come with me has to let me lead. You're not in the driver's seat—I am. Don't run from suffering; embrace it. Follow me and I'll show you how. Self-help is no help at all. Self-sacrifice is the way, my way, to finding yourself, your true self. What good would it do to get everything you want and lose you, the real you. (Luke 9:23–25 MSG)

The diamond is an exquisite gem, one of the most beautiful and valuable jewels in the world. Cut, clarity, carat weight, and color determine its worth. Just like diamonds, our personal facets reflect what is in and around us. When we allow sunlight to warm our lives, we sparkle and our radiance forces out the darkness.

My faith in God, love for Jesus Christ, and knowledge of the Holy Spirit have all changed over time. I spent my first twenty-one years of life in a small farming community in Northern Minnesota. My parents were hardworking, spiritually grounded, and respected members of

15

the church and community. I had three older siblings, all brothers, and I relished being the only girl and the baby of our family.

My childhood was typical and 1950s-simple. In my free time, I played loosely organized games of kick-the-can, hopscotch, "Annie, Annie I Over," marbles, and board games like Clue and Monopoly with my brothers and neighborhood friends. I could ride my bike with few restrictions, safely swim at the local lake, ice-skate with abandon on a frozen pond, play with my dolls in my playhouse, and visit my grandma and grandpa who lived down the street. Checking in at home occasionally was all that was required of me. Academics were not difficult for me. I loved elementary school and thought it was fun.

Even as a child, I knew I was born into a family of achievers. I was keenly aware of the unspoken emphasis on success and education. My three older brothers achieved academic success and some of my older cousins also modeled the quest for achievement. Praise flowed when success was visible and the family name was honored. My father was the mayor of our town and my parents were well known for their involvement in the community's charitable and political events. As the baby of the family, the expectations for me were no less, and during my elementary school years I measured up quite well!

At the age of twelve, my sunny, sparkly, and cheerful yellow world suddenly dimmed. Right before the end of my seventh-grade school year, I sat in my health class intent on acing my final examination. The classroom was painted a pale green, and a cool spring breeze blew gently through the open windows, moving the woven circular-shade pulls. The overhead light fixtures cast a soft glow while the radiator hissed quietly in the background. I diligently filled in blank circles on the multiple-choice final test feeling confident that I knew the answers. I recall thinking it was easy.

At the end of the week, I walked into the administrative office, retrieved my year-end report card, and brought it home. I never thought of peeking to see my grades. After my mom opened the report card and showed it to me, I was shocked! A huge red *F* was written in the column for my seventh-grade health class. I had failed seventh-grade health. I remember thinking, "Who flunks a health class?" I had no explanation for my failing grade. My mother was as puzzled as I was. She was not upset with me, but she wanted to know what had happened.

Within a few minutes of opening the report card, my mother put aside her homemaking tasks and together we walked the few blocks to the school and I entered my teacher's classroom. She was a young teacher and I never had a feeling that she disliked me nor had I received any feedback that I wasn't performing up to class standards.

I stood quietly in the background while my mother inquired about my grade. The teacher's quick and unemotional reply is still burned in my memory. Without a glance and with her eyes focused on work at her desk, she coolly stated, "Sara cheated during the final exam and I will not change her grade." I stood silently as words like *cheater* and *incompetent* were used to describe me. My input was not sought, and I was not bold enough to state my innocence. I felt hopeless. It was the worst day of my young life, and a turning point.

After what seemed to be an eternity but was probably ten minutes, the teacher made it clear that she had no doubt that she was right.

On the way back home I adamantly denied cheating. I am certain my mother believed me, but the damage to my spirit was irreversible and a battle with inferiority, low self-esteem and negative self-talk was born. Even as an adult and a teacher, I cannot define what it was that I did or did not do that brought on the accusation that I was a cheater. The language she used to describe me was branded onto my heart. I began to see myself as inadequate and stupid. I lost my love for school and I became an underachiever. I never worked hard at school again and became an average C-student who made an occasional *B*, and only one *A* for the rest of my academic career.

I felt angry and powerless. I had never had such a negative encounter in my life and at the age of twelve I didn't have the skill base or knowledge to know how to neutralize my emotional response. I panicked at the thought of tests, especially multiple-choice. I became paranoid whenever a teacher approached me and I wondered what invisible message I had sent. I questioned my ability and became sure that teachers did not see me as a competent student.

At the same time, my family was undergoing change, but as in any good Scandinavian family, feelings were not discussed. When we moved that summer to another Northern Minnesota small town, I had to take a multiple-choice math placement test. I did not do well and was placed into eighth-grade "dummy math" instead of the more difficult class. This reinforced my perception that I wasn't smart. My will to achieve academically became even weaker. Throughout four years of high school I seldom made the honor roll. I felt I could never measure up to family standards and expectations. I was blue, timid, insecure, and often lonely.

I knew I was expected to attend college, and did well on my ACT test even though it was multiple-choice. I loved the freedom college provided and the ability to choose my classes and discover personal strengths. However, that preteen fear of failure and rejection was still my companion. It seemed simpler to not try too hard, just enough to get by. In my mind, my brothers were great and I just *was*. I believed that I was a cheater, even though I knew it was a lie, and my self-esteem remained low.

Thankfully, I flourished when I could be creative and innovative. I blossomed in my elementary education classes and loved anything that had to do with language arts. My college professors found my enthusiasm for children and learning infectious and I usually received positive feedback. My perception that I mattered most when others found me attractive and fun fed my subconscious need for approval. I became a master at pleasing others in exchange for their acceptance. Like cubic zirconia, a man-made diamond, others' approval is nice, but it's not real and is usually fleeting. The synthetic stone will crumble under pressure and not pass the "scratch glass" test. Working hard for the approval of others is merely an imitation of the discovery of true satisfaction and happiness.

Even though I was raised in a home where biblical values were modeled and I knew about God's love and Jesus' death on the cross, these ideas were not personal for me. My childlike belief in "Jesus Loves Me" was replaced with teenage skepticism and an unspoken belief that God was the Big Tough Guy watching everything I did. He waited and watched so He could tell me how bad I was. I thought of

God as a "Make 'Em Work Harder and Knock 'Em Down" kind of guy. I kept a wary eye out for Him and the adults in my world.

My childlike free spirit was caged and although I didn't outwardly rebel, as a young woman I used alcohol to dull unpleasant feelings and often starved myself because I thought I was too fat. Although I did not become an alcoholic or develop a full-blown eating disorder, I teetered on the edge of both dangers.

As I pursued my elementary teaching degree and my first year in college, I fell in love with a young man I met on New Year's Eve. We were on our second date and going to a movie when he stopped his car to assist an old man who had driven into the ditch due to a snowstorm. I knew then that I had met someone special. Several months later he was drafted into the Marine Corps. He was sent to Vietnam and served ten months. Throughout this term, I wrote to him faithfully. Our romance grew into a commitment as we corresponded with each other, and our friendship deepened. We shared our individual hopes, dreams, and goals over those months via the mail. I felt that someone knew me for the first time and loved me in spite of my insecurities. After his honorable discharge, he returned home and we continued to date. By Valentine's Day of my senior year in college we were engaged, and we were married that summer. We moved to a community on the outskirts of the Twin Cities. God had blessed me with a very gentle and kind partner who truly loved me!

After five years of marriage our first child, a daughter, was born. Three years later, we received the gift of a son. I had many roles to fill in the subsequent years: mother, wife, daughter, sister, friend, teacher, housekeeper, laundress, and cook. We took our young family to church and I considered myself a Christian. I tried to be a good person, but somehow it wasn't enough. I began to feel a nagging sense of dishonesty. My life was good, but not great. My marriage was okay, but not passionate. My insecurities caused me to be a rollercoaster in my parenting and marriage. To state it simply, I believed everything in my life was gray and average. I wanted to dislodge this bleakness I couldn't even describe. After a while I felt it surround me, so I sought counseling. With my therapist's encouragement and compassion I began to examine areas of my life, to open up the garbage.

I started to journal the assignments I was given, which included opening childhood doors that I would have rather nailed shut. I revisited relationships within my family and discovered my need to forgive. I examined the expectations that I had internalized as a child and my inability to express closely held feelings. I began to more clearly understand my strengths and weaknesses. A wonderful thing happened: I learned that I actually liked myself!

My personal auditing included my sense of spirituality. My spirituality never grew beyond being baptized and confirmed in my Lutheran faith. Except for my simple childhood faith, I was stuck. I did not know that Christ wanted more for me than I could ever dream. My pain, insecurities, and fears that had been buried began to surface as I started to journal about these hidden parts of my soul. I spent time in prayer and started to believe that God might, possibly, love me.

For about a year I continued to receive counseling and I read my Bible in private. I read daily affirmations and devotions in the bath-

21

room before I went to my teaching job. Over time, I noticed a small, gentle change in my attitude and a feeling of lightness cracked into my personality.

Suddenly, I wanted more for my life, my marriage and my children. I wanted the gifts of love, joy, and peace to break into my gray world. Through reading the Bible, I learned that God created me and had a purpose for my life. I wanted to discover what that purpose was. I added the label "Believer" to my growing list of descriptors.

In the spring, I applied for a new position within our school district and before I interviewed, I copied out two Bible verses and put one in each of my shoes: "'For I know the plans I have for you,' declares the Lord, 'plans to prosper you and not to harm you, plans to give you hope and a future,'" (Jeremiah 29:11) and, "And we know that in all things God works for the good of those who love him, who have been called according to his purpose" (Romans 8:28). I knew that I would interview well if I portrayed confidence. I wanted to bring my real self into the process and that real self had a strong spiritual component. I knew if I relied just on me, I would not do as well, but if I relied on God and His magnificent power within me, I would be poised and self-assured.

I was hired in that position, and for four years I loved every minute of the growth and knowledge I received. I craved new experiences and sought opportunities to learn. I was convinced that God did have a plan for my life and I was secure in knowing that I would be guided. I went back to college and earned my Master of Arts degree in education. I received an *A* in all but one graduate-level class, which was sweet vindication for that insecure twelve-year-old girl accused of cheating who was now replaced with a positive and energetic woman!

Simple childlike trust in God brought the sunshine and sparkle back into my life. The qualities of a diamond replaced the darkness, fear of rejection, and low self-esteem I had experienced. The childhood labels of *cheater*, *dummy*, and *incompetent* became a faded memory.

Faith in God brought me a new kind of joy and I began to rejoice in being under His care and direction. My marriage gained new energy and my parenting style changed. My children and husband noticed the difference. They began to enjoy the happiness and peace from God that permeated our home. We raised our children by being engaged in their world. Whether it was sports or academics we encouraged them to try their best and know that we would be there if they fell and needed arms to catch them. My husband thrived and gained confidence and made good business decisions. He began to find comfort in his search for fulfillment too, and we became each other's best friends.

It amazed me that God's love was so deep. I realized I did not have to strive to do more or struggle with not having done enough. I didn't need to grapple with a lack of confidence and beat myself up, or search for human approval. For years I was a favored child in God's kingdom and life was good, so I was quite surprised and shaken when I began to struggle with personal commitments and a nagging loss of peace.

Around this time, I found myself finally unpacking books from our move. In those boxes, I found my journals from years back. As

I skimmed the pages, the same themes recurred: fear of failure and rejection. I thought to myself, "I want to be done with these weaknesses forever and ever!" But how was I going to accomplish this? First, I decided to dedicate some time to a daily walk, once a good habit but something I had abandoned in recent years. As I walked, I prayed to God for the gift of trust and obedience.

It was during these walks that I discovered I needed to return to my own personal garbage. I learned that an occasional trip to the garbage can wasn't enough. Just as we need to carry out our household trash daily, I needed to dump my personal garbage every day! I thought I had already dealt with all my trash and had received complete forgiveness, but once again, I needed to look at myself objectively. As I examined my life, my weaknesses and strengths, I realized that I had allowed stuff to accumulate and I needed a good house cleaning. I knew from experience that peace and joy would evade my heart until I was reconciled and restored, but this process was painful. God expected more of me than ever before.

One day, I ventured to our library book sale with the goal of finding inspirational music. But as I entered the building, I prayed that if God had a specific book in mind for me, that I might see it. As I browsed the shelves, I located the perfect soft-covered book, *Healing for Damaged Emotions*, by David A. Seamands. I paid the fifty-cent fee.

I devoured the book in one reading. One section described my struggle exactly: "Super You is a false idealized image you think you have to be in order to be loved and accepted. Super You is an imaginary picture of yourself. Since you have been programmed to believe that no one will love you if he gets to know the real you, you strive to become Super You, to gain love and acceptance." The author goes on to explain that by living up to others' unrealistic expectations, you take time away from developing your true self and a real relationship with God. If you waste your time pretending to be someone other than yourself, you won't heal or grow as a person.

I was reminded that in the process of self-examination, there is revival. I knew I needed to rid myself of those defense mechanisms I learned as a child. I needed to once and for all give up self-control to God-control. I knew that His greatest desire is to conform me to who I am in Him, and at that point, I began the process of being restored to an original work of art and my Lord's delight. One of my favorite Bible verses is:"How great is the love the Father has lavished on us, that we should be called children of God. And that is what we are!" (1 John 3:1–2). My spirit began to sing! During my waking hours, I would sing to myself the words from "Change My Heart" by Eddie Espinosa: "Change my heart, oh God, make it ever new, change my heart oh God, may I be like you."

I moved away from despair by lighting an imaginary candle whenever I felt a lack of trust in God. I battled with my trash by allowing God's light to penetrate my soul by reading, memorizing, and repeating Scripture. I focused on taking one step in the task assigned. I visualized myself as a shiny eighteen-wheeler barreling onto a writer's highway. I partnered with the Holy Spirit and gained the belief that I can be a diamond in His kingdom. God is ever faithful, and for my willingness to face my personal garbage, I was rewarded with a closeness we had not shared before. I realized that it is never too late to change and grow!

I know there is nothing better for men than to be happy and do good while they live. (Ecclesiastes 3:12)

Amen!

Action Plan

1. What desire has God placed in your heart?

2. Who might be placed by God in your life to be a guide and assist you as you courageously articulate and share your dream?

3. Ask yourself if you trust God enough to take the first step. If so, thank Him and begin. If not, come to Him with all your concerns in prayer. He will answer.

4. Write your action plan for finding the "Hues of You!" Begin by making a list of all of the colors in your life. What colors appear for you as you address areas of your life? Which areas do you value the most? Your list may include your goals and dreams, family, friends, work, and physical, spiritual, and emotional health.

Dreams and Grocery Stores

From my husband's Gideon KJV New Testament Bible: *The LORD is my shepherd; I shall not want.* (Psalms 23:1)

I was seven or eight years old when I had my first premonition. I entered the dining room of my parents' home, and my vision was drawn to the black rotary dial phone on the wall. I knew in a moment the phone was going to ring and that my brother had been in an accident and was in the hospital. Within seconds, the phone rang and my mother answered. My older brother had been duck hunting with a friend and had rolled the car and was indeed in the hospital. It was weird and something I didn't understand. I did not share my intuitive experience with my mother, but I knew instinctively that it was an unusual event.

As I grew older, I had premonitions several more times, but I learned it was nothing to fear. I reasoned that God must have designed me with this sense for a reason, so I just accepted that it was a part of me. Trusting this sense, I regard these incidences as calls to prayer, and they give me direction and encouragement. I am not alarmed by these rare insights; rather, I consider them a gift and perhaps a time to prepare for an impending rough spot. I am not sure why I have this heightened awareness, but I suspect more people have similar experiences and don't talk about them.

Frank shared with me that he and other Marine soldiers in his Vietnam unit had the 23rd Psalm written on their helmets and he wishes he had kept his helmet. While following orders, nineteen-year-old Frank was injured in an enemy ambush. As he lay wounded he saw his life flash before his eyes. Still, after many years and a Purple Heart, he quietly bears the emotional scars of war. He is tough, strong, and courageous—a man I am proud I married! In our years of marriage, Frank has had two serious illnesses, but before each sickness manifested any symptoms, I was forewarned.

The first incident occurred when our daughter was a senior in college and our son was completing his final year of high school and planning for higher education. Frank and I were just beginning to anticipate the "empty nest years," when a life-changing circumstance intervened. In the middle of a winter night, I had a realistic nightmare and in my dream I observed a three-legged man dressed in a white hospital gown with little paisley designs. This unidentifiable man was alone and rolling a cart toward a room where I understood he was going to have surgery. As I looked on, he unemotionally shuffled further toward the hospital's metal doors. Even though there was no dialogue, I knew in the dream that one of his legs needed to be removed and at the time of that realization, the taste of vomit filled my mouth and I awoke, my heart pounding. It was such a horrid sensation that I thought I must be getting ill. I wondered sleepily if there was any meaning behind the images or if it was just a case of severe indigestion that manifested itself as a nightmare.

I shared my dream in detail with my teaching partner and friend that morning and asked if she had any theory or explanation. Although she had no idea what it meant and was not accustomed to interpreting dreams, she suggested that perhaps Frank and I were disagreeing about an issue. Since my relationship with my husband was good and no concerns loomed, I brushed the memory of the dream aside.

Shortly after that incident, I was in the bathroom getting ready for school and I noticed bright red toilet water and drops of blood on the porcelain stool. I woke my husband and asked him about this very concerning sign. He dismissed the blood as insignificant, but I was adamant that it was serious. At that point, I felt the explanation for the dream was evident: Frank was ill. I made him promise to schedule a doctor appointment. Frank contacted his primary doctor and after a series of clinic appointments, Frank, who was fifty years old, was diagnosed with bladder cancer.

Several bladder scrape procedures were attempted before a more drastic treatment was recommended. Before his June surgery, Frank, his father, our pastor, and I had communion in our home and we placed our concerns at the foot of the cross. Frank underwent the seven-hour surgery to remove the cancerous bladder entirely and replace it with a neobladder formed from his large intestine. The cancer was diagnosed at stage three, but fortunately it had not penetrated the bladder wall or lymph nodes and there was no need for radiation or chemotherapy.

When Frank was transferred from the intensive care unit to a regular hospital room, the nurse on duty assured us that Frank would recover fully because he was in the "angel room." We asked what she meant and she said, "Look out the window and you will see!" I peered out his window. On top of the hospital's heating and cooling unit, I observed the clear and sharply defined five-foot outline of an angel—complete with wings and a halo—formed from rust and peeled paint. The nurse explained that every patient who was assigned to this particular room with the angel nearby had done well. The room was a blessing indeed! With adjustments to lifestyle, Frank's prognosis was excellent, a wonderful outcome to my ominous dream.

Twelve years later on a beautiful March day, Frank and I stopped at a grocery store close to our rented vacation home in Naples, Florida. He waited in the car while I did some quick shopping. In line at the express lane, I struck up a conversation with the friendly woman beside me. The checkout line dwindled and we laughed and continued our chat as we exited the store together. She knew I was from the Midwest because of my accent, and asked where we were planning to attend Easter services. I told her that our plan was to be at The Villages for the month of April. Before we parted, she invited us to her church for a Sunday service and offered to give me a card with the address of the church. To be polite, I waited while she retrieved the card, but I thought of Frank, who I suspected was getting impatient. As she searched her somewhat disorganized car, she informed me that she was an outreach evangelist for her church.

Frank was parked directly across from her car and I could see him glance in the rearview mirror, likely wondering what I was doing.

I shared my reluctance to wait too long while she rummaged around and finally, as she handed me the card, she gently touched my forearm and her exact and assuring words were, "You need to know that your husband is going to be just fine! His heart is being softened right now!" I assumed that she was referring to his occasional impatience with me. I thanked her and returned to our car.

Several days passed and Frank's mother, sister, and brother-in-law arrived for a visit. Frank had a terrible night. He tried to sleep, but he was restless and sweated so severely that I needed to change the sheets twice. Finally, after taking some Tylenol he fell asleep and I slept on the living room couch. The next morning, March 25th, he stumbled out of the bedroom. He was unable to control his severe shaking and I announced, "We are going to the clinic!" His mother zipped his shorts while I helped him button his shirt and tied his shoes. Our brother-in-law drove us to the urgent care clinic several blocks away and when we arrived Frank's temperature registered 104.5 degrees. He was still trembling.

Because of his bout with bladder cancer, he is susceptible to infections. The attending physician diagnosed a severe bladder infection and treatment began with an hour-and-a-half IV infusion of antibiotics. The next day at his follow-up appointment, his blood still showed an infection and hospitalization was recommended. His care was transferred to an internal medicine physician and infectious disease consultants were also contacted. We were 1600 miles from Minnesota and our only option was to trust this unknown medical system. Frank's mother and brother-in-law flew back to Minnesota the next day, but Frank's sister extended her stay to support us.

I was concerned, but not alarmed. I felt that he was going to be okay and that the bladder infection would be healed. Frank was hospitalized in the lowest level of care and was able to function quite normally. We went for walks through the corridors and bought him ice cream treats. When he was visited by the hospital clowns who made balloon animals, he thought that was too much and found their humor more nauseating than the medicine he was required to take. I knew he was fine because he was getting testy. "You need to know that your husband is going to be just fine!" appeared accurate.

Even though he'd been so ill, Frank did not want to return to Minnesota or change our plan to spend April in The Villages. By Friday, after being hospitalized for four days and receiving antibiotics, we were told his blood tests came out clear and his infection was gone. The staff told us the infectious disease specialist saw a "hint of something" in his intestinal area on the abdominal CT scan, but we were given the okay to continue with our vacation. We filled a bucketful of prescriptions and left the hospital with the recommendation to follow up with his personal physician when we returned to Minnesota.

Frank, my sister-in-law, and I, arrived at our rental villa at The Villages, Florida, on April 3rd. Friends had eagerly awaited our arrival and planned a night out, so after unpacking at our new residence we met them for an enjoyable meal. Our evening concluded and we slowly meandered outside, unwilling to break up the reunion too soon. Our waiter sprinted after our group as we visited on the boardwalk. He pointed to us and informed Frank and I that we had not paid our dinner bill. I had assumed that Frank paid with our credit card as usual before we left the restaurant, but he hadn't. This was odd and something we would never intentionally do, but I assumed it was just a silly mistake due to the excitement of being around good conversation and good friends.

The next morning was Sunday and since we agreed the worst was behind us, Frank's sister returned to Minnesota. Frank and I decided a few staple items would be good to have, so we drove to the grocery store. Inside the store, Frank suggested that we purchase pork chops and grill them like we had the previous night. I couldn't believe what he was saying, and he seemed so mixed up. I asked him a few questions, and found that he had forgotten at least three things. He did not remember we were in The Villages. He did not remember eating out the previous night, and he did not remember we were disappointed because this rental property didn't have a grill. His disorientation upset me and I cried right in the store. I felt powerless and vulnerable and thought he must be having a diabetic something-or-other, since he had been recently diagnosed with the preconditions for diabetes. Then I tried to tell myself we were both just exhausted from the previous health scare, but I truly didn't know what was going on. A phrase nagged at the edges of my mind as we quickly left the store: "You need to know that your husband is going to be just fine."

I was unsure of our next step. I questioned our decision to stay in Florida and thought about how to get us back to Minnesota.

Should we drive home? Is this more than just being tired? I prayed that God would help me figure out what to do.

As we entered our home, the phone rang and my prayer was answered. The caller was a friend with whom we had dined the last evening. She had been seated closer to Frank than I was during dinner, and had noticed something I had not. She told me Frank seemed quiet and withdrawn, not his usual jovial self who loves to tell stories and jokes. Her concern had prompted her to call a doctor earlier that morning to explain her concerns. Based on her consultation with the doctor, she thought Frank should go to the emergency room. I expressed concern that Frank's many experiences with doctors and hospitals usually mean he's hesitant to seek care unless he feels it's unavoidable, and that it might be difficult to get him there. She offered to come over and talk to him. Soon our friend and her spouse arrived and surprisingly, without much persuading, Frank agreed to go to the hospital. On the ride to the ER, Frank demonstrated more confusion. He seemed uneasy and childlike.

As Frank was questioned by the triage/intake emergency nurse, he began to glance around the small, enclosed area. He appeared distressed and his blue eyes were empty and glazed. He knew his name and birth date, but was totally confused about where he was and why he was there. My usually strong and confident husband appeared helpless. The nurse asked me how long he had been like this. I replied frantically, "This is just happening now!"

"No," she insisted, "I need to know how long this has been going on. It's very important!"

I told her about his confusion at dinner and in the grocery store. I stated I had never seen this blank and confused look before. Within seconds, Frank was placed on a gurney and received emergency care. I returned to the reception area where our friends and I prayed together. Soon, I was asked to return to the emergency room and the doctor on duty informed me that Frank was exhibiting signs of a seizure and needed a scan.

Meanwhile, his vital signs were a concern and to calm him he was placed into a medically induced coma. I was allowed into the sterile, gray, stainless steel emergency room and held his hand as he lay on the blue gurney covered by a thin white blanket. I became a bit-player in the scene while nurses and doctors rushed around me attempting to make order out of the chaos occurring in Frank's body.

As he underwent the MRI of his brain, I watched from behind a glass wall and heard the results and diagnosis of a brain tumor and possible hemorrhage. I was present when his breathing tube was inserted and blood spattered across his sanitary white hospital gown. Whenever I was given the opportunity, I kissed his cheek, stroked his head softly, and told him how much I loved him. In retrospect, I am surprised that I was allowed so much access to him at this time. Even though he could not hear me, I sang "Jesus Loves Me" very quietly. I reassured him that everything was going to be just fine. Those words echoed in my mind constantly.

I was asked if he had a living will, did I have power of attorney, and finally, did I know what his wishes might be? I needed to give verbal permission for intubation because his breathing was stressed and uneven. I nodded *yes* to everything and signed all the appropriate papers, but Frank's needs soon exceeded the hospital's capabilities. He was transferred by ambulance to the trauma center thirty miles away. It was suggested that I contact our children. All of this happened within one hour of our arrival at the emergency room. The words, "You need to know that your husband is going to be just fine!" returned to my mind.

I was surprisingly calm throughout the scene and felt that God was in control. I planted my husband and myself firmly in His care. I didn't have a Bible or anything to hold physically in my hand, but I did have silent prayers going at all times. I also had an 800-number for twenty-four-hour prayer listed in the planning calendar in my purse. I called the number on my cell phone and when they answered I asked them to pray for my husband who was very ill. I gave them his name and before I could add more, I was called back to the emergency room. I knew the friends who accompanied us were praying in the waiting room. I felt our situation was covered.

I was not allowed to ride in the ambulance, but time was a blur as I was driven to the trauma center. I contacted our children and told them that their dad was very ill and in a coma. I informed them about the brain tumor and his vital signs. They were on a flight from Minneapolis to Orlando by 7 o'clock that evening, and they arrived at the hospital around midnight, less than twelve hours from the grocery store incident. We watched helplessly as Frank struggled to maintain life. It was a great relief to be surrounded by family in this terrible circumstance and we stayed by his side throughout the night and day.

Specialists were consulted and Frank was placed under the care of a neurologist. There was a flurry of commotion and quick decision-making. Our daughter, who is employed at Mayo Clinic in Rochester, communicated with physicians back home. Her coworker, a nephrologist in the transplant center, offered to coordinate Frank's care between Florida and Minnesota. Frank would fly home to Minnesota for treatment, but he would not be released for transport until he improved significantly.

Even in the trauma center, Frank continued to have focal seizures. We believed everything was under control, so after being up for many hours my son, daughter, and I returned to our rental villa for a night of rest. In the early morning we called the hospital and the nurse on duty suggested we come in as soon as possible because the night had not gone well. When we arrived we were told that the incorrect dosage of medication was given and Frank had suffered multiple seizures for hours. The doctor on call and in charge of his care would not answer her phone messages and because they could not contact her to receive her approval to change the dosage, the correct amount was withheld. The smaller petit mal seizures escalated into grand mal seizures, which continued through the night. Finally, the intensive care unit night nurse intervened and broke protocol by consulting with another physician. The correct medication was administered immediately and Frank began to respond, but the process of monitoring him was intensive. Later, the on-call physician apologized, but stated she had been sleeping so soundly that night that she did not hear her phone ring.

At this time I felt, "You need to know that your husband is going to be just fine!" did not appear to be correct.

We were furious when we heard what he had needlessly endured. When we entered Frank's room that morning we saw that his hands were strapped to his bed so he would not pull at the multitude of tubes. His tongue was swollen because he had bitten it during one of the grand mals. He was confused, anxious, extremely agitated, and thought he was back in Vietnam. He was frustrated and perturbed by everything, especially me. He looked at me and demanded that I find his *green* sweatshirt. He wanted his *green* sweatshirt and nothing would calm him down. Our son tried to convince him that the green sweatshirt was in the closet with the rest of his belongings. Sometimes I would leave his room in tears because we were all so helpless to soothe him in any way.

On April 8th, the fourth day of our Florida ordeal ended and a new one began. Frank was to be airlifted home to Minnesota. Before we could proceed, I needed to pay for the flight in advance because our insurance would not cover the costs of a flight until later. I needed an instant infusion of cash into our checkbook, so I called my brother who wired funds into our account. Two nurses staffed the plane, and the pilots flew the six of us to Minnesota. We arrived at the hospital by ambulance from the Rochester airport and Frank was whisked to a critical care unit. Doctors from several disciplines were called in for consultation.

The Mayo Clinic pieced together a startling list of diagnoses, and the chain of events that was revealed reminded me of the children's story of The Little Red Hen and her dilemma of locating the right resources to assist her as she baked her bread. We were more fortunate than the motherly chicken, and were able to get some help along the way. Everything had to happen precisely as it did for all of these problems to come to light and for Frank to be able to receive the care he needed. Fortunately, instead of a fictional chicken, Frank was a real tough bird! First, Frank may have had a bladder infection, but the first Florida CT abdominal scan's "something" was a duodenal perforation that had caused urosepsis in Florida. The infection in his blood was caused by an undetected intestinal ulcer, the ulcer and high temperature may have caused the brain hemorrhage, the brain hemorrhage set up the swelling, and the swelling brought on the seizures, the seizures then led to the discovery of the six-centimeter lesion on the lining of the frontal lobe of his brain.

After the final diagnosis was determined at the Mayo Clinic and surgery was a viable option, his doctors suggested that Frank return to Park Rapids and allow his body to heal. He was placed on anti-seizure medication and we drove home with guarded optimism. We were extremely relieved to be back in Minnesota and home.

"You need to know that your husband is going to be just fine!" Those words became my unspoken mantra before and during Frank's surgery. When we met with the neurosurgeon after the five-hour operation, he appeared exhausted. He stated it was a tough surgery. There had been more "fingers" of the tumor than expected and one area in his brain was a particular concern. We would know the extent of any brain injury in recovery. He also told us that Frank had 105 metal stitches extending from ear to ear across the top of his head.

Our children and I held our breath as the attending surgical nurse tested his leg and arm movements as well as his mental acuity. We held our breath as Frank, with a bandaged head, responded to all oral commands. He could move his arms and legs and wiggle his fingers and toes. He knew where he was and why he'd had surgery. He recognized us and winked confidently. The chief neurosurgeon at Mayo Clinic described Frank's health journey with one word: *miracle*! I exhaled, feeling that I finally understood what I'd been repeating to myself the whole time, "Your husband is going to be just fine!"

Prayer, friendships, family, and faith were the adhesive that held me together in the eye of these medical storms. From the first prayer in the Florida emergency waiting room with friends to Frank recognizing the smell of alcohol on a cotton swab after his surgery at Mayo Clinic, our family brought our troubles to the Lord. He was faithful and comforted each of us while bringing healing to my husband. Prophetic encounters can be a gift and I know the two incidences concerning my husband refreshed my heart with the knowledge that God is in control.

The second part of my grocery store acquaintance's message was that Frank's heart was being softened, and indeed I see it every day. His gentleness and emerging gift of patience are genuine and his great love for his family is authentic and a core value. His memory of what happened is limited due to the tremendous stress his brain was under, but his love for others and his thankfulness to God for giving him another day is a miracle we are all thankful for and can enjoy. I am quite confident that now he would consider giving those aggravating hospital clowns a great big hug!

Surely goodness and mercy shall follow me all the days of my life, and I will dwell in the house of the LORD for ever. (Psalms 23:6 KJV)

Amen!

Action Plan

1. Model healthy habits. Schedule an annual checkup and insist that the men in your life receive one too.

2. Prepare a living will and have it on file at your health care facility. You do not want your children, spouse, or other family members to be put in a position of guessing what your desires might be.

3. Visit or volunteer at a hospital or nursing home to provide comfort and companionship for people who might not have friends and family.

The Quilt Called Friendship

Do not be anxious about anything, but in everything, by prayer and petition, with thanksgiving, present your requests to God. (Philippians 4:6)

F riendships are like quilts that cover us and keep us warm and comfortable. The varying colors, textures, and pattern choices make a homemade quilt an interesting piece of art, and they often become a symbol of our heritage that is passed down for generations. Lois was my best friend and one of the most beautiful people I ever knew, but her outer beauty was surpassed by her inner beauty. Her radiant smile, interior decorating sense, and gentle personality were some of her trademarks. Through life's seasons for twenty years we were faithful confidants. Lois was a large piece of my quilt.

We shared many similarities: we were both originally from small Northern Minnesota communities, and I was only fourteen days older than she. We both married the summer after college graduation and we began our teaching careers in the same elementary school, where our classrooms were across the hall from each other.

Although we knew each other socially for years, our relationship grew into a true friendship the year we were offered district-wide assignments. Lois became the Elementary Art Coordinator and developed art-based curriculum for our entire district, and I was hired as the Staff Development Coordinator. Our new offices were located next to each other. As two elementary teachers in the middle of monumental jobs, we began to rely on each other for encouragement, advice, and a ready ear. Over the next four years, our relationship developed into a deeper friendship and we also shared our faith journey. Lois' desire was to help me strengthen my faith and advance God's will for my life. Lois became my prayer partner and she was always available to listen, pray, and give me a hug. She shared my joys, sorrows, pain, and triumphs.

We loved teaching next to each other and often collaborated on creative lessons for our students. We both enjoyed being innovative, and we worked well as a team. Lois was the detail person who could figure out how to do what we wanted to accomplish while I was the fun person who thought of ways to incorporate activity and spunk into our teaching. One of our favorite projects was when we built a spaceship out of large cardboard boxes and covered it with silver paper. For several years we had our fourth-grade students learn about the fifty states in social studies by researching, writing, and putting on a play to teach an alien named Lexicon who had landed in our classroom by mistake. Lexicon was the most sought-after role because he/she came out of the capsule dressed in green and wearing an old snowmobile helmet. We kept the children focused on learning, but the positive interactions between the students and us were also important. When I see students from those team-teaching years, they still recount the fun they had in our classrooms.

While I believed classroom pets were important for my students and usually had a hamster, Lois didn't really enjoy them. But, one year she decided to have a miniature rabbit as her classroom pet, much to the dismay of the janitor. Her son had gone back to college and the pet was left at home. The rabbit liked to suck and nibble on her students' sleeves, and her kids often went home with shirts that had holes chewed in their cuffs. Every weekend she would either find a child to take the rabbit or else she would need to bring it with her. That only lasted one year, but I can still remember the bunny in its lovely basket in the back of her classroom.

Over the years, we developed a daily routine of taking turns driving through McDonald's to bring a good cup of coffee for each other in the morning. Sometimes we could not remember whose turn it was and we ended up with a caffeine high from drinking two cups! We finally switched to purchasing cups of half real and half decaf because we got so mixed up.

One day, Lois was introduced to consignment shopping. Because she had an excellent sense of style, she could find exceptional name-brand buys and her wardrobe grew to include expensive designer clothing, purses, and shoes purchased at a much-reduced price. She instinctively knew which colors worked for her and she often wore orange, khaki, and sage green, but brown was her color. She not only wore it well, she painted her townhome's accent walls brown too. I remember once I came to her home and when she opened the door she was wearing a pink jogging suit. She had always taken the adamant position that she *could not* and *should not* wear pastels—it was one of her strongest opinions. I actually laughed so hard, I almost peed my pants because I had never seen her wear pink! I never saw her wear that color again.

Lois was like a much-loved aunt to my children and she watched them grow into fine adults. She sang at both of their weddings as well as other special family events. Lois shared her beautiful singing voice many times while visiting my mom. She sang old favorite hymns to her while I sat nearby with tears streaming down my face. As she ministered to my mother softly with her music, she was sharing another unique part of herself. Lois beamed when she sang songs of faith.

As Lois and I shared our journeys in faith, we were able to encourage and support each other by attending inspirational events together. One time, we decided to take a special trip because Lois had heard about a speaker from Canada who was scheduled to present at a suburban church near the Twin Cities. Her call to place our reservations must have been timed exactly right, because we were invited to an intimate morning gathering with the speaker.

The morning of the event, we drove separately. In the privacy of my car, I prayed for release from a sin that lied heavily on my heart even though I had asked for forgiveness many times. I met Lois at the elegant lake home and together we entered. It was my first adult experience of participating in worship and praise outside of a church setting. It reminded me of the private meetings in homes the first disciples of Jesus Christ must have held as they tried to avoid persecution. Although I was unaccustomed to this type of event, the setting was serene, friendly, safe, and made me feel comfortable.

Our speaker led about fifteen of us attendees in worship songs and accompanied us on her guitar. After a few minutes of harmonizing, the presenter stopped singing and announced that she had received a message for someone named Sara. My heart began to pound! Was *I* the Sara? I felt put on the spot, and my mind raced to the worst scenario. Was I going to be asked to leave for some reason? I raised my hand timidly, as if I were a reluctant student, and my stomach dropped to my feet.

"God has a message for you," the speaker said. "New things and new ways to worship will come to you. I am your future and present. All things have passed away, all things are new." She paused to pick up her guitar and continued, "Sara, God wants me to sing this song to you." Everyone in the room was mesmerized. It was truly one of the most dramatic moments in my life. She sang:

> *I am your God.*
> *You're as free as a butterfly smelling the flowers.*
> *Do not worry; I have healed your broken heart.*
> *Rejoice in me—I have set you free.*
> *You're my butterfly.*
> *I will always be with you.*
> *Something new will come to you*
> *and shall fill you with my joy, peace, and love.*
> *You are my butterfly.*

Lois also received words of encouragement at the luncheon. Her message included walls being broken down, which was welcome news because she was in the process of getting a divorce and had many burdens. Lois was also told that she would be "filled with joy and dance with a tambourine." We rejoiced in the news that there was healing in her future. I was speechless and amazed.

At lunch, Lois and I ate our turkey sandwiches as if an encounter like this was commonplace; however, we couldn't wait to reflect on our day together in private. Later we giggled like young girls. We had stumbled together into another exciting activity! We often shared our amazement that what one of us wouldn't dare do alone, we would find strength to do together and we became more adventuresome! The following Christmas I gave her a tambourine as a reminder of that powerful day. She hung it on her study wall.

At the end of the school year, we decided to spend a Saturday morning together attending a presentation on the spiritual gift of discernment. This was another instance when we had no idea what we were really doing but trusted our friendship to do something together that we wouldn't do alone. The topic was new to both of us and we had never heard of the Prayer Ventures organization before. We sat together in rapt attention during the morning's lecture, and at the conclusion of the session, individual prayer was offered. People who were requesting prayer were instructed to raise their hands. I felt my heart throb in my chest like never before, *ka-boom—ka-boom—ka-boom*. I whispered to Lois that I thought I was supposed to raise my hand. She encouraged me, and with the sound of my heart still pounding in my ears I put up my hand.

A woman joined us and introduced herself as a prayer partner. The three of us sat together on the hard church pew. We bowed our heads, held hands, and prayed for me. This was the first time I had ever had anyone other than Lois pray for me. As we prayed, I felt warmth and I sensed a blue light in my body near my right ovary. The sensations of warmth and the color blue continued for a few seconds and then disappeared. My heart had stopped pounding and I felt warm, safe, and loved.

"I need to tell you something." In the car I recounted to Lois my experience with warmth and blue light within my body. I specified that I thought it was on or around my ovary. I shared that I had been having pain in that area for several weeks, but I hadn't mentioned it to anyone nor had I made a doctor appointment. I thought it might resolve on its own, so I didn't get it checked out. I have never had a serious health concern, but I had mentally given myself another month to wait and if it wasn't gone, I resolved to make an appointment. However, every time I sat down, I felt something uncomfortable. I had developed a habit of edging my body carefully into a sitting position as I did when I entered her car that day, but there was no pain. It was just gone. Lois shared that as we prayed together, she had felt her hands tingle and her fingertips became warm. Later we discovered that those two sensations are often present in a healing from God.

Over the next several years, Lois and I continued our spiritual growth together. We took classes, attended retreats, and participated in prayer training. Lois was a gifted prayer warrior. She strengthened her commitment to healing prayer and became a learned student. Eventually, she accepted the position of Prayer

Coordinator within the Prayer Ventures organization and became a strong advocate for healing through prayer. Lois' many talents were a great asset, and she added a special quality to the group.

Time passed and Frank and I retired to Park Rapids, Minnesota, and Lois moved to Maple Grove, Minnesota. Although we were further apart than before in miles, we talked by phone once or twice a week and frequently visited each other. Our friendship didn't miss a beat.

One summer day, I drove to the cities to meet Lois for a day at a spa, a very belated Christmas gift we had given each other the year before. During her yearly mammogram in July, two suspicious lumps had been found in her left breast. Lois needed to revisit the clinic before our appointment that day. It was then that she received results from the biopsy. The lumps were indeed cancer. Upon hearing the news, Lois seemed calm and not alarmed. Instead of going to the spa, we went back to her home and I cried all the way there. I think she would not permit herself to cry because she needed to be strong, so I was her emotion that day. She said, "Oh Sara, you are crying for me because I can't!"

Lois had many dear friends and all of us were devastated by her diagnosis. But Lois was confident and very wise. She asked seven of her friends to each take a day of the week and be her prayer partner. On the designated day, the prayer partner would either visit her at her home or pray with her by phone. I was her Monday partner and every week for months we talked and prayed and cried together on Monday. Lois read books on healing, ate a healthy diet, attended her weekly prayer training sessions, and continued to live her life in spite of cancer. She was determined that cancer would not define who she was.

Lois and I maintained steady communication via phone, but I also kept up with her updates on CaringBridge.org. In one entry, Lois wrote the following: "Early this past Monday morning, I woke with the sense that I needed to 'label' this time of my life. I could not understand why—in my not-fully-awake state. However, my mind was running through all kinds of words like *recover, renewal, connections* and the like. Suddenly, it seemed that God placed 'swing' in my mind. Asking for clarification along with the visual, I sensed the words 'Firmly planted...eyes heavenward!' I realized that quite literally God is my 'swing.' I am firmly planted in His care. I am to rest in Him and enjoy the thrill of the ride! Isn't that a cool perspective?"

Because an MRI later showed that the cancer had spread to the perimeter of her breast, chemotherapy was recommended to shrink the cancer before a bilateral mastectomy. Lois followed the treatment and had surgery as planned. She arranged to have private prayer with family before surgery, and during her surgery friends prayed in the chapel of the hospital the whole time. I arrived to lend a hand for a few days after her release from the hospital. Together we measured the fluid discharge and carefully bandaged her chest area to reduce the swelling and control her pain. We laughed, cried, played games, and prayed. She continued to have visits with her daily prayer partners and I witnessed the affection and esteem that these friends felt for her.

It hurt her to laugh too much so we had to be careful about what topics were "safe" and would not make her sore. We couldn't reminisce about past misadventures where her lack of a sense of direction got us into some pretty shady parts of Minneapolis and St. Paul. (I still don't know why she wouldn't listen when I told her she was going down a one-way the wrong way!) We couldn't discuss our varying viewpoints on politics because we found it funny how opposite we were at times. We had often laughed and enjoyed our differences and found humor in our everyday experiences. Even the simple fact that I always ate all her chocolate chips when I visited and she didn't have any left for cookies brought smiles and giggles. All through her treatments and recovery, I took for granted that my friend would soon be healthy and sharing our inside jokes wouldn't hurt her anymore. I never questioned the possibility that she might not rally and fully beat this terrible disease.

While in treatment, Lois' sense of style became an ongoing topic at her doctor appointments. It was not unusual for her to wear a chic hat with matching sunglasses enhanced by her dazzling smile. Lois thought of hairlessness as just another opportunity for creativity to shine. When she visited the hospital for treatment, the nursing station would light up because they wondered what snazzy outfit she would wear. Lois had a strong faith and her resiliency and adaptation to her new "normal" was inspiring. Lois continued her education in prayer ministry and also pursued her passion for design and decorating. I assisted her as she helped decorate a church for a women's luncheon. She transformed a stark and dull fellowship hall into an inviting and thoroughly charming space. Even though she was still undergoing treatment she continued to serve others.

Lois was delighted to become a grandparent during this time and spent several weeks in Colorado with her family that spring. She loved her grandchild with all her heart and felt blessed by his birth. She found it very difficult to leave her grandson and return to Minnesota, and the thought of moving to Colorado was planted in her mind.

Lois continued her fight and contended with the effects of radiation and more chemotherapy, but healing was evasive. The following months brought devastating news. Her cancer remained aggressive and treatments were not changing the course of this dreaded disease. Lois decided it was time to move to Colorado to be closer to her family. This took time and effort while her stamina was declining. Many obstacles needed to be overcome, including the problems of insurance and locating a new physician and clinic. However, because of her inner strength and tenacity, she was able to work through all the details. She even shared her talents within her new church in Colorado, beautifully decorating their fellowship hall for a birthday party in the honor of a woman she never even knew!

I was heartbroken. I was unable to attend the open house she had for all her friends before her move to Colorado and that made me even sadder. I slowly began to realize that her ultimate healing would occur only when she was brought into the waiting arms of Jesus. We talked very little about her impending death, but we both knew it was the outcome unless God brought healing to her body. I held onto that hope until the day she died. I don't know what exactly happens to a person at the point of death, but I imagined my friend completely restored and fully enjoying her heavenly surroundings.

During her time in Colorado she gained a network of new friends through The Gathering Church and their loving support was extended to her entire family. Lois' children made the commitment to care for her at home. With the wonderful assistance from another close Minnesota friend, family members, and hospice, Lois was able to be home with her children and grandchild while she received palliative care. The warmth of love from each of her caregivers pervaded her room. Lois' acceptance of her death brought comfort to everyone; in spite of the tears that were shed, there was a definite sense of peace surrounding Lois and her family.

We kept up our communications and talked even when her voice was weak and speaking became a chore. Lois embraced everything she had ever learned about prayer and drew closer than ever to her Savior. While my family coped with Frank's health scare in Florida and the subsequent surgery, I called her and asked for prayer because I was secure in her desire to help me in any way possible. It was exactly what I would have done at any time during our relationship: turn to her for strength. Even as her physical strength waned, her love and compassion were the same as ever.

We prayed together daily and held together across thousands of miles. She told me she had a vision of Jesus and his angels surrounding Frank during his hospitalization at the trauma center. She said she knew Jesus stood at the top of Frank's head where the medical equipment was placed. As her death approached she continued to lift others to the Lord in prayer, a powerful witness.

In spite of the fact that Frank just had surgery, I made arrangements to visit Colorado when her death became imminent. I couldn't let my friend go without a final visit. I needed to tell her in person how much I loved her and how she had enriched my life. Another dear friend arrived and as we sat by her bed and rubbed lotion onto her fragile skin she said, "I feel so loved!" And she *was* loved.

I spent three days in Colorado by her bedside. When I first arrived she was able to communicate, but every day she became weaker. On the day I had to fly back to Minnesota, I put my head on her bed and cried silent tears as she slept. Lois lifted her hand and gently patted my head, feebly whispering, "Strength and comfort, Sara, strength and comfort." Those were the last words I heard her say.

Lois died that spring at the age of sixty-one. Her two-year battle was over. Of all the jewels, gems, and precious metals found on Earth and in Heaven, Lois is among the finest treasure to touch my life. At first, comprehending that my best friend was gone was only possible when I visualized her securely embraced in the arms of her Savior in Heaven, dancing with her tambourine or swinging on a swing. Lois' heart's desire was for all glory to be given to God. His faithfulness was evident throughout her life and that is what she wanted to be remembered. Lois would not want me to place her on a pedestal. She was human, but was a treasure to those of us who loved her as well as in the eyes of her Savior. That is also how God perceives all His children who love Him.

A dear friend who visited Lois two weeks before her death recounted a conversation with her and wrote down their end-of-life discussions. I was given a copy of their exchanges. One topic was based on John 14:2, "In my Father's house are many rooms; if it were not so, I would have told you. I am going there to prepare a place for you." One of Lois' dreams was to decorate the townhome she had planned to purchase in Colorado. When it didn't look like this was going to be possible, Lois smiled and said, "God may need me to decorate for Him." Lois got very excited and animated while talking about this. If Jesus went ahead to prepare a place for people, she said, each place would need to be unique for each person and the decorations would need to fit their style and personality. The Bible says that Heaven's gates are decorated with pearls, city walls are adorned with jasper, sapphires, emeralds, and topaz, and the streets are pure gold. Lois thought all the jewels and gold were, "a bit over the top." She laughed and quipped, "God is so gaudy. He could use a little help."

When asked by her friends shortly before her death what she would say to her children about life, her answer was: "You need a deep faith. Rest your life on three foundations: faith, family, and truth. Bring God into the mix of your planning. You learn to take small steps of faith; then you are ready to take the big steps."

Lois, my dearest friend is gone and I miss her. But, I am also reminded that her earthly struggle is over. I am lifted up as I think of her faith and trust in God, and just as Lois and I were always more daring when we were together, I find more courage, strength, and comfort as I remember her. She always challenged me to be the person God intended me to be. The "Lois" patch in my quilt remains, helping to warm me. My memories of having had such a close, strong friend are stitched firmly in place.

Amen!

Therefore do not worry about tomorrow, for tomorrow will worry about itself. Each day has enough trouble of its own. (Matthew 6:34)

Action Plan

1. Become a light to someone who is grieving or dealing with an illness. Visit or send a hand-written note. We are often uncomfortable and don't know what to say, but the words are less important than the meaning conveyed by your presence or a kind thought shared.

2. Ask yourself if you need to grieve. Give yourself permission and begin the process. Journal your thoughts and become aware of your internal messaging.

3. Write a short note to your special friends and share with them how they have positively influenced your life.

4. Volunteer with cancer fund-raising or become a hospice volunteer.

Forested Back Roads and Mud Puddles

Arise, shine, for your light has come, and the glory of the LORD rises upon you. (Isaiah 60:1)

This verse from Isaiah was a gift. It helped me realize that God's love is without boundaries. It came to me at a time when I lacked trust, obedience, and confidence in God and it seemed impossible that God would empower me, through the Holy Spirit, to move beyond my fear, anxiety, and depression.

I love my Polaris 400 Sportsman four-wheeler and enjoy driving it through the logging trails in Northern Minnesota. There is nothing better than maneuvering my powerful-enough-for-me machine through the forested and swerving back roads. I carefully guide my four-wheeler over bumpy rock-covered hills, and I merrily splash through mud puddles. I make quick-thinking turns to avoid unexpected wildlife or fallen trees and branches that block my way. When all four wheels are on the path, everything is in control and working well. *Danger* and *fear* are not in my vocabulary. I'm just out in the woods having fun!

The four-wheeler symbolizes the journeys in my life. Before Lois' passing and Frank's health complications, I coped well with my obligations and the many roles I played. My wheels were all on the ground and life was good. But in the space of six months, my wheels started coming off the path and I operated in fear and trepidation. My husband faced a life-threatening illness, surgery, and a slow and painful recovery, and my dearest friend was gone. Two more friends passed away in the span of a few months. One friend died from breast cancer a few weeks after Lois died. Another good friend, our son's godfather, passed away after a three-year battle with brain cancer. In addition, eight months earlier Frank's father had passed away and the family was in the process of selling the farm. Disagreements arose, as they will in all families, and this added to my stress and increased my sadness. At best I had two wheels on the ground and the mud puddles that used to be fun to splash through began to look like impassable swamps.

Even though I had so many blessings in my life, I did not feel grateful. I teetered on the brink of depression. I did not have the time, or desire, or will to grieve as deeply as I needed to for the loss of my best friend and the changes in my life that were happening so quickly. That was a mistake. I was agitated, crabby, and unhappy. I was unpleasant to my husband and insufferable to be around. I moved out of our bedroom and into the loft. I couldn't stand being around anyone and that included my husband. I was angry that he didn't understand me. I thought he should be able to sense my unuttered feelings and do something. He ignored me. I am sure he thought, "Best to stay out of her way!" I was in what I would characterize as "the dark night of the soul." I was lost, alone, afraid, sad, and angry. These negative emotions wreaked havoc in my brain. I tried to pray, but even prayers were forced and cold. Many nights I could not sleep, and I developed a habit of being awake from midnight to three o'clock a.m. after I'd gone to bed. I did everything required of me. I cooked the meals, I did the laundry, I responded to needs when asked, all without any joy in my heart. Eventually, I navigated through my days without emotion. It hurt too much to let myself feel anything. Gradually the tools of prayer, friendship, walking with Jesus, and keeping an optimistic attitude disintegrated and I would not admit I needed help—not even to myself.

I fumbled through months of living in this dark room with a single beam of light streaming through the only window with its shade pulled halfway down. I kept up outside appearances and my behavior looked good to others, but I was a mess inside. No one knew how sad, lonesome, and devastated I was. As I reflect, I am sure that the beam of light coming through the window was God's love and presence, but I could not bask in it for relief. God seemed far away. The spiritual part of me appeared to have died when my friend died. My marriage felt broken and I felt discontent with life. Nothing was normal anymore. The time we spent with our families, which would usually make me feel energized, left me exhausted. I pretended to be happy and cheerful, but inside I was seething with irritation. I believed that I didn't belong to anything that really mattered. I wanted to be left alone.

Since sleep was evasive, I concentrated on reading. I turned to what had helped me in the past. I found strength in God's word and read Scripture in various translations. I devoured books on emotional healing and the Holy Spirit's role in our lives. I wrote my thoughts and throughout the early morning hours I discovered God's help was critical to move forward. With God's assistance, all the accumulated trash could be incinerated. God was nudging me toward making a decision: either I commit every area of my life to Him or I retain the ones I didn't trust Him with and suffer the costs of self-sufficiency. I knew that if I continued on this path, I would continue to struggle.

One morning as I read, the verse from Isaiah 60:1, "Arise, shine, for your light has come and the glory of the LORD rises upon you," stood out on the page. I repeated it in the days ahead. God affirmed that verse again within a few days when it appeared on my online devotion from godsminute.org. The closing paragraph states: "So Sara, it is my prayer that you are already walking in God's Glorious Light! If not, now would be a great time to start! Ask God to fill you with it. For you will find that to be a truly wonderful experience, and don't worry, though God's Great Light is brilliant, it is guaranteed not to give you a sunburn! Now may you have a bright, sunny day that is filled with God's Love! Amen."

During the summer, that verse came into focus frequently. I held onto it for dear life and claimed it as God's intimate message for me. It became a common experience for me to discover how it applied to my normal twenty-four-hour cycle. I researched various phrases in the verse. What did "the glory of the Lord rises upon you," mean?

If *arise* meant to get up and get going, could *shine* represent God's action plan? What was God directing me to do?

I have been a hospice volunteer since our move to Park Rapids. During this time of suppressing my grief and being in a depressed state, I needed to attend a hospice training session. In addition to God's gift of the Bible verse, the training day was the beginning of my healing. As part of the session, each participant was requested to share a loss in their life and also their coping mechanism for dealing with the loss. Each woman told her story with emotion, and in the sanctity and unspoken empathy we all felt for each other, healing tears were wiped away. I was unable to verbalize my loss because of the lump in my throat. The wounding of my heart was too fresh. At break, I shared with the hospice trainer our losses and family health concerns. This person listened and didn't judge my emotions right or wrong or suggest ways to fix the situation. It was the first time I had verbalized how much I missed Lois and how very lonesome I was.

Another gift that day was a handout that included "Searching For Myself," a description of what happens when people experience a loss:

> Someone once said that when grief picks us up it never puts us down again in the same spot. We move. We change. We are all that we were before, plus the experience which has hurt us, plus the new individual who emerges to cope, and to move on. And so our neat and predictable lives become our past, and our present is always expanding in new directions...One of the most important tasks of grief is

the re-organization and re-identification of self. What have I lost and who am I now? (Author Unknown)

When I read this, I instantly understood that part of the grieving process is adapting to the change. This was a huge insight and I realized that I could mourn without being detached. I had been taught since childhood that only positive emotions should be verbalized. Any negative emotions should be buried and, as a coping skill, you should think about all the people in the world who have it so much worse than you do. Well, that wasn't working for me.

"This is overwhelming," I thought to myself. I began my quest to empty my garbage can and progress from inaction to action, from lack of purpose to fulfillment, and on to chasing away unhealthy thinking with encouraging and positive thoughts. I needed help! I investigated the possibility of working with a life coach. I contacted a delightful woman, a life coach, who has authored a memoir of her own healing. I had met her previously at a presentation at our church, and my heart was desperate to begin the restoration process. We met and discussed coaching and her first question was, "What makes you feel plugged in? What gives you energy?"

"When my will is aligned with the will of the Holy Spirit I switch into high gear and my wheels are on the ground. I am unstoppable unless I run out of gas. But I am currently grounded!" I answered. I was still coming up with the right answers, but the very core of me was empty. My gas tank contained just a drop of fuel. My wheels were not all making contact with the earth. After answering a few more insightful questions, I revealed my desire to write about my garbage can and diamonds experience.

"Why haven't you written it yet?"

I explained the lack of support and multiple reasons why I could not write a book, but it wasn't true. How can someone support you if you don't share the fact that you need help? I valued independence and self-sufficiency so much that I seldom showed any weakness. Asking for help is akin to being weak and I was not going to admit that to anyone! I did not tell her that my lack of trust in God caused my inability to move beyond a basic introduction over twelve years. I did not share that my desire to write was hobbled by a severe lack of confidence. I did, however, explain that I felt like a boulder was tethered to my leg with a leather cord. I explained that the rock's weight was limiting me. I did not have the energy or the tools to budge the boulder. I am not sure what she thought of the rock, but she didn't laugh.

Over the summer months, I took small steps to overcome fear and restore the belief that God did have a purpose for my life. I wrote my thoughts and feelings, I walked, I read my devotions, I prayed, I connected with family, and I was gentle to myself and gave myself permission to *feel*! I forgave myself and I became more loving to my husband. I began to be honest about my needs. I knew my journey would include telling the story of my search for God's love, forgiveness, tenderness, direction, and finding my diamond, but I had to unload the garbage first—a terrible and smelly job.

I cut, with God's and my coach's help and an imaginary scis-sors, the leather band that attached the boulder to my right leg. It astounded me when I realized that the one factor that held me hostage was *me*. It wasn't my husband. It wasn't the lack of moral support from friends. It wasn't my ability. It wasn't any of those things. My lack of trust in God kept me stuck and unable to move forward. In fact, the dream of writing a book stayed a dream and after twelve years it became a reminder of all I was not doing. As weird as it is, once the rope attached to the rock was slashed, the stranglehold I felt disappeared. I was free to move forward. I tentatively shared with a trusted friend my desire to write. She didn't laugh either, but instead encouraged me to continue to look in that familiar garbage can. She suggested that I might want to go to a hermitage where I could have solitude, be nurtured, and write. I called the retreat center and one cottage was available for the week I requested.

I disappeared from life and experienced the hospitality of The Dwelling in the Woods for nine days in October. I left my home with my clothes, bedding, four translations of the Bible, several daily devotions, a Bible study guide, my computer and printer, a cell phone, and a critical supply of Peanut M&Ms. I also brought my cross inscribed with Psalms 138:8:"The Lord will fulfill his purpose for me; your Love O Lord, endures forever," and Lois' brown shawl. I printed a copy of my online devotion with Isaiah 60:1-2 and I thought I included a picture of a dove my life coach had e-mailed me to represent the presence of the Holy Spirit.

The surroundings were beautiful, tranquil, peaceful, and conducive to beginning to write about my life experiences. There were miles of well marked walking trails, beaver ponds, a labyrinth to wander in contemplation, and a library and resource center. The main building housed the staff, and the kitchen was stocked with healthy food. Two days' worth of meals were prepared and available to pick up. Their famous freshly baked bread was a bonus! I couldn't have been more supported.

My one-person cabin was perfect. It sat on the edge of the property overlooking a small pond, and several feeders outside my window attracted birds throughout the day. A dove decal on the window was placed above the small round table that served as my desk. I was thrilled about this as I unpacked and realized that I had left my dove photo at home. I displayed my cross and a copy of Isaiah 60:1, and my little area was all set up for writing. I thought, "How cool that God is in the details!"

When I arrived, I wore jeans and a nice top, makeup, and gold earrings. I went to bed at my regular time and listened to Minnesota Public Radio for twenty-four hours. Sleep was still elusive, but I was not worried about it. I made frequent calls to friends and family, assuring them that I was having an okay experience. I went for walks and attempted to find my way through the labyrinth. I was so focused on which way to go that I never said one Bible verse or prayer. I thought the twists and turns were a bit corny. When I reached the center I looked around and thought to myself, "What's the big deal?" and followed the path out. I thought some great insight would appear, but I remained the same, no big "God thing" happened.

By the third day, one-third of the way through my stay, I noticed a change. I no longer bothered to apply mascara or lipstick. I placed my earrings in a bowl along with my wedding ring and watch, and I turned off the radio. I played a few of the CDs I borrowed from The Dwelling in the Woods' library.

I had also packed a CD of Lois singing hymns. I had tried to listen to it at home, but I always turned it off. I was afraid I might get too emotional. But in the solitude and safety of the hermitage, I became courageous. I placed Lois' brown shawl around my shoulders, lit a candle, read my Bible and daily devotion, and sat in the rocking chair. Then, I turned on the CD player and listened. I sobbed, but soon the deep sobs became soft, gentle and healthy tears.

The next days were wrapped in silence in my little cabin. I did not need any outside stimulus and I kept my own hours of wakefulness and sleep. Because I had only me to take care of and was free from the usual clamor of daily schedules, I was able to write unhindered. If I wanted to write, I approached my computer and wrote regardless of the time of day or night. Soon I had written the core of what I believed to be important. I was accountable to myself and I began to find the joy of just being me. My connections to my regular life became less frequent and I mostly corresponded through e-mail with a few friends with whom I shared my latest writing. I knew in my heart that I was not supposed to do that, but I was so excited about my journey that I didn't listen. Finally, I had to write at the top of my pages: "Do NOT send out!" I began to take pleasure in rediscovering the truth: God loved me, I am a cherished child of the King, Jesus Christ is my best friend, and the Holy Spirit would give me direction and comfort!

The day before I was scheduled to leave, I decided to walk the labyrinth once more. I picked up a stone I had collected during a previous outdoor walk and brought it with me. This time I became more thoughtful and enjoyed the journey. This time, navigating the twists and turns became a joyful process. I sang quietly and repeated my Bible verse. When I arrived at the center, I placed my stone in the pile of rocks, dried flowers, and twigs that previous visitors had used to form a cross. I left the path and returned slowly to the real world. As I exited, I rang the bell over the entrance as a symbolic gesture of the conclusion of this part of my journey.

After my walk, I decided to do a bit of laundry. I rested in a large overstuffed chair in the office area, and while I waited for my first load to wash I visited with another "hermit." I found out this young woman had graduated with a degree in religion and was voted "Preacher of the Year" at her Canadian college. In the course of our conversation she asked me why I was there. I told her I was there to begin the process of writing a book, and she expressed her sense that she, too, would like to write about her walk with God. She was recovering from the loss of her fiancé who was a volunteer physician in Haiti. He had been recently killed in a car accident while helping the hurricane-devastated country. She was also grieving the loss of her father to a prolonged illness.

That night in my cabin I sensed I should offer to meet with this beautiful young woman before I left. I talked to the director, her friend, in the morning and I volunteered to meet with her at noon. I could share my process and perhaps encourage her heart and spirit. My offer was readily accepted and we met and talked for an hour. We prayed and cried together as we blessed each other. In that short time, I learned that an open and friendly heart is seldom turned away, and to trust that my story would reach women of all ages, just as her story will. I learned that age is not a barrier and all women have hurts and need healing for their wounds. I discovered that just as my hospice friend listened to me, I could fulfill that role for someone else. We never exchanged more than our first names, but I empathized with her desire to reorganize and identify this new person she became when her losses began to define her.

At the end of my nine days of quiet spiritual caretaking, I packed my car for the journey home. I was dressed in jeans and my nice sweater with my earrings and other jewelry in place. Mascara and lipstick completed my look. I met with the personnel and thanked them for the gift of time and the wonderful, caring atmosphere. I was given several good recipes as a parting gift and was encouraged to contact them when I had further needs or was ready to unveil my book or lead a workshop. I drove down the driveway and onto the asphalt highway back to my world, but I was changed. I was all that I was before my experience, but I felt more complete and renewed. The anger had disappeared and my life consisted of a desire to fulfill God's purpose.

And a highway will be there; it will be called the Way of Holiness. The unclean will not journey on it; it will be for those who walk in that Way; wicked fools will not go about on it. No lion will be there, nor will any ferocious beast get up on it; they will not be found there. But only the redeemed will walk there… (Isaiah 35:8–9)

Amen!

Action Plan

1. If you can, get away from your regular life (even if it's only for a few hours) to examine who you are, what you want to accomplish, and if you are on the right path.

2. Talk to a trusted person about your goals and what you think might be holding you back. You might consider working with a professional life coach.

3. Imagine what your obstacles might be, then visualize yourself defeating them. Light a torch to see down a dimly lit path. Build a fence to keep out negativity. Stand up to your inner saboteur and send her packing.

4. Write out your goals and brainstorm how accomplishing them would make you feel.

5. If you are depressed, don't try to deal with it yourself. Contact a medical doctor, a counselor, a pastor, or even a good friend to help you get well again.

The Cross and the Good News

For God so loved the world the world, that he gave his only begot-ten Son, that whosoever believeth in him should not perish, but have everlasting life. For God sent not his Son into the world to condemn the world; but that the world through him might be saved. (John 3:16–17 KJV)

To Christians all over the world, the cross is a symbol of Christ's death and the tremendous price he paid for our sake. When Jesus was crucified, a painful and humiliating way to die, he took all my sins upon himself and created peace between God and myself. I know that as a believer, I am a much loved and cherished child. "I will be a Father to you, and you will be my sons and daughters, says the Lord Almighty," (2 Corinthians 6:18).

The cross is a simple form made of two beams, but it is a magnificent representation of love. The vertical part of the cross reaches toward Heaven, but it is anchored in the earth. As faithful followers of Christ we are expected to live in the world, but not be driven by external values and earthly desires that might lead us to abandon our true calling. Our goal is align ourselves with His purpose and will for our lives. We are to receive encouragement and direction from our Heavenly Father through the power of the Holy Spirit.

The horizontal section of the cross represents God's wide-open arms, which are always ready to receive us. His outstretched arms invite us into a relationship where we will find nurturing, protection, and love. The prodigal son, who returned home beaten down and full of self-hatred, was welcomed back by a father who had a forgiving heart and arms that wrapped his wayward child in love. God's arms are similarly extended to invite us into a warm and loving relationship, not because of who we are or what we have done, but simply because He loves us.

When I struggled alone in our loft at night to find recovery and restoration, I decided to challenge myself to observe crosses in my environment. This search became an important step in my healing and helped to build my self-confidence because it brought the message of God's love to the forefront of my mind. I have a cross that is printed with Psalms 138:8: "The Lord will fulfill his purpose for me; your love, O Lord, endures forever." I moved it front and center on my writing desk. I started and ended my day with that Scripture verse. Besides the cross in our study and the one Frank made for us, the next crosses I "collected" were in our home. We have large windows overlooking the lake, and their construction forms three crosses that are easy to see. The tallest cross is in the center, just like on Calvary. Guests often comment that our home is warm and inviting, and I think it has a lot to do with these subtle symbols.

Strolling through the woods I connected with nature and noticed how tree branches also form crosses. I suddenly felt like everything was magnified on my daily walks because my environment appeared full of wisdom. The Minnesota state tree, the Norway pine, is prominent in our area and is an impressive symbol of God's great sacrifice. The pine tree's main trunk creates and feeds branches on both sides, forming a cross. These branches nourish more limbs, and the limbs supply food to the needles. The needles, positioned along the sides of each branch, also create multitudes of miniature crosses. Before we retired from our jobs, Frank and I contemplated where we would make our retirement home and our realtor brought us to a beautiful piece of lake property. Frank and I revisited the small parcel of land and we held hands and prayed for guidance under a pine tree. We eventually purchased the property and constructed a log home out of local Norway pines. I adore living in the midst of these strong trees, an ever-present reminder of God's beauty.

Searching for more crosses on the hills and pathways to the Heartland Trail, a beautiful biking and hiking trail close to our home, I was in the midst of God's creation. Everything, including the scent of clover, the wisp of butterfly wings, the flight of the songbird, or a strategically placed mushroom, surrounded me with nature and I gained inner strength and felt very close to God. God reminded me that He was the Power and all of nature appeared to be resonating with His love for me. I became emboldened.

I was not alone in renewal. Frank, who had retired five years prior, began to create projects in his woodworking shop, where he quietly began his own unique ministry with the cross symbol. The first cross he made was patterned from one my uncle had given my mother years ago. He started making them as baptism gifts for our grandchildren, but now goes into production several times a year and gives them to family and friends as gifts. His gentle spirit and faith are evident in each cross. Beginning the process with roughly sawn pieces of lumber, much of it from trees we cut down to build our home, Frank challenges himself to make each cross unique. They vary in wood variety, size, style, and stain color. I think the cross represents God's gift to him and is a visual symbol of God's love. When his father, Kenneth, passed away, Frank placed a cross in his casket as a symbol of God's love for his earthly father.

Recently I taught a class at our church for parents of teenagers. On the last night of class, I brought a basket full of Frank's homemade crosses to give to the parents as a reminder that God is in control and He loves those teenagers with all His heart. Two teenage boys were in the classroom when I entered, and thankfully they offered to help me set up the video equipment. They saw the crosses in the basket and to show my gratitude for their help, I inquired if they wanted one. The boys beamed as they both picked out their favorite. I used this opportunity to talk with them about the symbolism of the cross, and they quickly caught on to the meaning behind the vertical and horizontal beams.

At the closing of the class, I shared our experience of raising two teenagers. For parents it is a time fraught with worry and apprehension. My concerns for my children were brought to the cross many times. I know my children were sometimes testy rascals, but God protected them throughout their search for independence. Most importantly, because I believed that God cared for our children even more than I did, I was able to relax and sleep at night. I suggested to the parents that they ease their own anxiety by physically holding the cross in their hands and praying for their children.

In difficult times, our prayers take on an urgent tone and the cross becomes even more of a comfort than usual. When Frank needed to have brain surgery to remove a tumor, I packed a cross as a comforting reminder that God was in control. Before our children left the hospital to get a night's rest, we prayed as a family. We prayed for the doctor's skilled hands, peace and healing for Frank, and strength and courage for us as we waited. We searched for place to put the cross in the waiting room, and finally settled on a popcorn bowl. The mood lightened as we held hands and laughed at our makeshift display. Even this everyday object could be transformed into a place of honor. God didn't mind one bit! The natural disturbing thoughts of all that could go wrong and projection of the "what-ifs" about the surgery faded away. With Frank's cross nearby to reinforce my strength, I told myself that faith is an intangible personal trait and a gift to be received. It was then that I became mindful of my sense of peace and lack of fear and apprehension during this emotionally complex time.

Because I learn best by sight, I use visualization in my prayer life. I imagine myself slouched at the foot of the cross, irritable, exhausted, discouraged, and dragging a trash bag. This garbage bag is full and heavy! I couldn't hoist it off the ground if I tried. My bag contains a mélange of innocent slights from others that I brewed

into a larger issue, my tendency to gossip, my habit of procras-
tination, and a multitude of other sins. I slowly remove the bag's
twist tie. Without any enthusiasm, I dump the reeking contents at
the base of the beautiful wood cross and remember this passage
from Colossians 3:13: "Bear with each other and forgive whatever
grievances you may have against one another. Forgive as the Lord
forgave you."

The evidence of my guilt is laid out before me, and I know that if I
want forgiveness, I must forgive. If I desire the characteristic of love,
I must exhibit love. I feel a gentle breeze, and my individual pieces of
trash float away. The flight of each bit symbolizes a lightening to my
spirit and I am refreshed. Soon all of my garbage is whisked away
and the magnificent blue sky and wispy clouds are all that remain.

I notice that I am barefoot and attired in a thin white dress. There
is a large baby-blue silk scarf around my shoulders. I take the scarf
off and swish it in the air. I hear music and I begin to dance—the
scarf and I are one, swirling and twirling at the base of the cross.
Soon I am dancing with graceful moves in a beautiful pattern. I am
light, happy, and free, not the grumpy and despondent woman who
arrived here.

A gust of air lifts the scarf gently from my hands. It drifts toward
the horizontal crossbeam and drapes the cross with flowing beauty.
I am aware of the smallest details of my surroundings, and am in
awe of Christ's death on the cross for me. Instinctively I know it is
time to leave. I quietly and serenely back away with my head bowed
reverently and tears of thankfulness filling my eyes. I am refreshed,
restored, and at peace. The invitation to return to the cross at any

time is open-ended. I am encouraged to return with a bag full of garbage, a basket full of worry, a prayer request for a loved one, or with just simple childlike faith and a thankful heart.

Amen!

David wearing a linen ephod, danced before the Lord with all his might. (2 Samuel 6:14)

Action Plan

1. Place a cross in an area where it is readily visible and reflect on its meaning.

2. Consider this passage: "For the message of the cross is foolishness to those that are perishing, but to us who are being saved it is the power of God" (1 Corinthians 1:18). How can the power of the cross translate into your life?

3. God uses numerous means to speak to us, including through our senses. You might find God when listening to music, enjoying a bouquet of flowers, patting a puppy's soft fur, or sharing a delicious meal with friends. How might sight, sound, smell, touch, and taste assist you in your faith journey? How will you deliberately utilize your senses during your worship time?

My Mom, Pillsbury Doughboy, and China Teacups

Those who look to him are radiant; their faces are never covered with shame. (Psalms 34:8)

It was a spring morning and as I prepared to write my mother's eulogy, I poured some coffee into one of her fine china cups. I chose a teacup decorated with a hand-painted robin among white and pink apple blossoms and went outside to sit on our sunshine-flooded front deck. I thought about my mom and her collection of china teacups that she kept in an antique glass hutch. My mom had the gift of hospitality and she served coffee, cookies, and a favorite sweet bar with affection to her honored guests, including the hearing aid salesman as well as her pastor. She held everyone in high esteem. When visitors arrived for coffee, my mom would open the cabinet with a black key—the one we kids knew we couldn't touch—and bring out her best cups. When my family and I cleaned out her home after her death, there were only two teacups left. She had given most of them away to her caretakers as a token of her gratitude for their attention and care. As I sipped my coffee I reminisced about my mom, her life, and the values she held dear.

My mom's parents were some of the first settlers in Pennington County. My grandfather and his parents immigrated to the United States from Norway in 1893. Together with his father, he operated a steamboat on the Red Lake River. My grandfather met my young Norwegian grandmother when she cooked for them on the boat, and when she was sixteen they married. When my grandpa told his father he was marrying my grandmother, my great-grandfather asked him where they were going to keep her. My grandfather replied that she was so tiny she could sleep in his dresser drawer. As a child, I loved hearing that story. When I asked my grandmother about marrying so young, she said she would do it again, but would not recommend it to me!

My mom was the third of twelve children and she loved the out-doors her entire life. She helped her father with the farm chores and often drove their team of horses with the milk and cream to the creamery. My mom left home after completing the eighth grade and worked in various homes as hired help. One summer, she returned home to assist the family and was in a field pitching hay. My dad, who was delivering fuel oil, saw her and thought she was quite lovely. Another young fellow was interested in her, but my mom always had the desire to be a missionary and wasn't particularly interested in getting married. Luckily, my father was a persistent suitor and at the age of twenty-eight, she and my father were mar-ried. They were active in their church and the small Minnesota com-munity where my father operated the gas station, and they became parents to four children. When I was a preteen, my brother, parents, and I moved seventeen miles north, where my dad owned and operated a grain elevator. During the busy fall days at the grain company, my mom would help my dad by nailing boards in the railroad boxcars before the grain was loaded. She could accurately hit a nail on the head with either hand.

My mom was forty-one years old when I was born and I always thought she was old and not "with it" as some younger mothers appeared to be. Perhaps one of the largest impediments to a strong mother-daughter relationship was my fear of my mother. I loved her, but I was afraid of her too. When I was a four-year-old, I had done something wrong and my mother spanked me. She asked, "Sara, are you going to be good?" I answered, "No!" This happened repeatedly until she became so exasperated that she dragged me into her bedroom, put me in the closet, and shut the door. I don't know how long I sat in the dark closet, but to a four-year-old it was a long time—time enough for me to learn that I was bad, my mother didn't like me, and I was pretty much alone. As I grew older and was expected to help with housework, I was a "scatterbrain" and could never remember the correct placement of things. I could never remember if the glasses in the cupboard should be bottom-side-up or top-side-down. I could not remember which rugs went where throughout the house and often mixed them up in a way that I liked better. I drove her nuts.

Because my own internal messaging system was flawed, I wasn't a very kind teenager and my insolence often made her cry. But, she tolerated my young-adult disregard for her values. She accepted my adult self-righteousness. When I went off to college I started to smoke cigarettes and drink alcohol. She found my behavior offensive, but never preached to me and continued to do what she did best: reach out to God for support and encouragement. I know she continued to pray for me. It wasn't until I had children that I began to appreciate my mom for her wonderful qualities, and when I became a believer, my regard for my mother increased exponentially. I recognized that my mom's background and insecurities defined her as much as mine defined me. We had a very healing conversation and a warm and healthy reconciliation where we both forgave each other. As I learned to overlook our differences, I began to value her obvious talents. I learned to love and cherish her as much as God loved and cherished me. All parents will make mistakes, but it doesn't have to be a permanent chasm. Mutual respect and perhaps even a joyful relationship are possible.

One of the things I learned to cherish about my mom was her sense of simplicity. She did not need a lot of frills to be effective and she loved the challenge of creating something out of nothing. If she thought an article of clothing could be remade into something useful she would not throw it away. Her quilts for World Relief were made from discarded fabric or castoff clothing. Because of her commitment to God, life, with all its unpredictability, was never really complicated for her. My mother was an uncompromising worker who made an effort to bring God into all she did. Her faith and her commitment to keeping things simple included her love of sewing and her skill in creating exquisite handiwork.

When I was a child, I wore some of the sharpest tailor-made clothes, most of them made from castoffs. She would take apart secondhand garments and craft them into lovely fashions for me using her treadle sewing machine. One of the coats she created for me won the coveted "Grand Championship" ribbon at the county fair. As a teenager, I was never in want for stylish clothing because if I described something to her, she could make it, even without a pattern. One winter, she made me a black seal fur jacket that I adored and wore all through college. It was warm and sustained me through several cold Northern Minnesota winters and it signified her love for me. My mom sewed my wedding dress and a bridesmaid dress on her old sewing machine while she took care of my very ill grandmother.

For my sixteenth birthday, my parents bought me an electric Singer sewing machine. She was not interested in learning anything about the zigzag stitch and she never attempted to learn how to sew on my machine. She liked the simplicity of her faithful treadle, trusted crochet hooks, and pointed knitting needles.

My mom also knitted sweaters for me and taught me how to knit. The first item I made without a pattern was a tan wool sweater. I just followed my mom's instructions and it turned out great! She crocheted the most beautiful piece of art in the form of an eighteen-inch doily, which is framed and on center stage in our home. It is such a difficult pattern that even the most skilled artisan would have a hard time reproducing it. She made this pattern for all her favorite people and mine has blue thread on a darker blue background. The basic pattern is the pineapple design and the cocoon stitch.

That stitch in itself is beautiful and complex. At one time, my mom was offered money to write the pattern and sell it, but she declined. Guests marvel at its construction and I am captivated every time I study it. I am amazed when I recall that she made this beautiful work by studying a small, unfinished piece that someone gave her knowing she could figure it out.

Sentimental and unfailingly loyal to those she loved, my mother saved every message, card, and note her grandchildren wrote to her. When my dad could no longer drive she drove him around for hours in the afternoon. She loved my husband and thought he was one of the most special people in the world. If I ever complained about him, she would say, "Well, you knew that when you married him and he is a good man!"

I thought about how she would often say, "I was just thinking of you!" with a pleasant smile, and she always meant it. I recalled that she brought her apple cider vinegar and water mixture onto the plane when she flew to visit my brother in Pennsylvania. She drank that concoction faithfully for years. I remembered her visits to our home and her wonderful help. She loved to clean, and my refrigerator, stove, and floors shined when she left. Toward the end of her traveling days, she attended my son's high school graduation and in preparation we cleaned and polished everything. She was missing after a while and I found her outside on our deck scrubbing between the boards with a toothbrush. Oh my goodness, she was funny!

Even now I chuckle when I see The Pillsbury Doughboy in a commercial. Although he is just a trademark character for Pillsbury, my mom loved him. Doughboy is a fixture on their products and has been around for years. He is adorned with a chef's hat with the Pillsbury logo, two round blue eyes, a beaming smile, hands with thumbs and no fingers and a gentle poke on his tummy makes him giggle. I am not sure if my mom liked their products as well as she liked the little guy, but she only purchased Pillsbury flour for her baking. Whenever Doughboy was on the television, she would put down her crocheting project and watch his brief spotlight. She smiled and chuckled along with him. I can't read any more into her enjoyment of his personality except for the fact that my mom, as creative and talented as she was, was also very blessed with the ability to enjoy the simple things in life, like this charming bread-dough pitchman.

When my parents retired, they lived a fairly active life until my father became ill. My mom cared for him at home for several years until he passed away. After his death, she resumed her life and hobbies. She returned to making her fall pickles, rolled lefse, and baked Norwegian flatbread, relaxed with handiwork, and helped others. Mom lived independently in her home, did her own housework, and traveled to see relatives from Alaska and Pennsylvania.

Flowers and vegetables flourished under my mother's care. Before most people knew what *organic* meant, my mom was a very successful organic gardener. Her gardens were unsurpassed in beauty. She supplied neighbors and family with produce throughout the summer and her flowers adorned the church altar for Sunday services. She got rid of weeds in the sidewalk by pouring boiling water on them and fed spoiled bananas to her thriving houseplants. Every fall we would rake the leaves and trench them in the garden, and she composted everything so that the soil was rich with nutrients. She loved the seed catalogs that arrived in the winter and she painstakingly planned what new variety of lily or other flowering plant she would grow. My own attempts at gardening were feeble compared to hers, but the spring before her death, I had my best and most beautiful flower garden. Before I visited her on Mother's Day, I walked down to my garden, the same one where I noticed my missing bracelet, and there among all the gorgeous colored flowers was one absolutely stunning white lily. I knew in my heart that God placed it there just for my mom. I picked it carefully and brought it to her with love in my heart.

At the age of ninety, her health and her memory began to concern us. Throughout her decreasing mental and physical status, Mom's temperament remained calm, kind, and caring. However, her capability to cook, clean, and care for herself was lost. She fell numerous times, suffered several small strokes, and developed heart disease. Her memory loss was obvious. We realized that the harsh Minnesota winter was not far away and Mom was no longer safe by herself. We hired caregivers, but before her ninety-first birthday the decision was made to move her closer to my home in Buffalo. I vividly recollected the day my brother and I brought her to her new memory-loss home.

The colorful maple leaves in our front yard, the crisp September air, and the cloudless blue sky did not lift my spirits. Our mission to move Mom into a homecare facility designed for women with dementia and/or Alzheimer's disease was not going to be easy. The evening and subsequent morning conversations with my mother to tell and retell her of our plan to move her closer to her children took continual effort. Together we packed several suitcases with her clothing and personal items. Memories of my mother, as well as my childhood, were everywhere. I knew she would never be back to the home she loved. The home where I grew up would be empty.

As a coping skill to her memory loss, my mother displayed favorite pictures of family members on the kitchen table, taped them under the cabinets, pinned them onto the curtains, and perched them on the windowsill. Her photographs and the memories they represented were priceless to her. I gently packed these pictures that had become a bridge to a past that was fading from her memory.

We needed to leave by noon. My mother's new home and four housemates waited 220 miles away, but she refused to leave. Mom sat in her favorite orange flowered chair and would not budge. My brother and I were ill equipped to deal with her rejection. Every emotion stirred in my heart and we were at a loss to know the next step.

When Uncle Helmer came to say goodbye, he assessed the situation accurately. He gently knelt beside my mother, held her hands, and said, "Emma, you need to go with your children. You will never be alone, because God is watching over you." He prayed a short prayer and tenderly hugged her. My mother got up, put on her coat, and said, "I want to walk through the house once more. Then I'll be ready."

Within a few minutes my mother was seated in the front of the car next to my brother. She commented on the cloudless blue sky and the fall colors. I sat in the back seat as silent tears trickled down my face. I prayed for all of us.

The last eighteen months of my mother's life were lived near me in Buffalo, Minnesota. Every time I came to visit, which was daily, she asked if she could come home with me. She tried to escape through the locked door and refused to sleep in the bed provided. I found her on the floor in her bedroom more than once. She became combative with the staff and within a few weeks we were advised to locate another care option. I could not take care of her at home, but there was an opening in a home setting for memory-impaired women and we had the option of placing her there or in a nursing home. After my brother and I had met with personnel from both places, we instantly decided to move her to Cherished Moments. She became one of five female residents in a home-based facility for women with Alzheimer's or severe dementia.

It was a wonderful decision. During those months I watched with fascination as her love for Jesus continued and her gentle personality resurfaced. She modeled poise, compassion, and charm in spite of all her losses. As she dined with the other memory-disabled women, some of whom had forgotten how to hold a utensil or even swallow, she held their hands and helped them eat. She read the Bible daily and as her cognitive abilities diminished, she gravitated toward a child's edition. Eventually, she began reading her Norwegian Bible. She continued to make simple knitted items, and I would visit after teaching school and sit with her as I corrected my students' papers. She was always interested in what I was doing.

It was difficult to experience the first set of circumstances, but once our mom received the wonderful quality of care from Cherished Moments, our lives were enriched. I learned a new appreciation for the talented caregivers who loved my mom almost as much as we did. I also learned firsthand about the overwhelming sadness of losing a parent to cognitive impairment. As her strength slowly ebbed, my mother decided to stop eating and refused to take fluids. Her bed was moved to the solarium. Surrounded by windows on three sides, my mother who loved to garden and enjoy the outdoors could be enveloped in nature's beauty. It seemed quite appropriate to spot a diminutive robin on the railing outside the window by her bed. The little bird was watching her intently when I came to sit with her, hold her hand, and read her Bible verses. Shortly after that, my brother and I witnessed my mother's entrance into Heaven.

It took time for me to appreciate, love, and honor my mother, but fortunately I did learn and that time was a gift. I thank God for giving me my particular parents, especially my mother. She modeled for me a grace-filled life. She was unique and out of touch with the world's definition of success and beauty. She was not well educated and was somewhat of an introvert, but what she valued was clear in her kind actions toward others and concern for their needs. She was my significant source of prayer and never-ending love. Her prayers, I believe, were for me to become aware of God's love and to know in my heart that I am first and foremost His child.

My mom learned early in life to commit concerns to her Savior and then to let go. She represented a life lived with total dependence on God. She remained firm in her faith that He would supply her needs. Because she didn't desire to please others, she possessed a sense of peace. Her strong faith quietly defined her.

I found a beautiful handwritten message about the definition of faith in her Bible: "Faith is a gift from God, who has dealt to every person a measure of faith. Faith is that characteristic of the soul that brings you in contact with God. Faith is the only avenue to God. Faith is the thing above all else that pleases God. Faith is the assurance of things hoped for, the evidence of things not seen." Then she had copied down Hebrews 11:6, "And without faith it is impossible to please God, because anyone who comes to him must believe that he exists and that he rewards those who earnestly seek him."

I sipped from the china teacup and was brought back to the real world by the sound of the phone ringing. I left the sunshine and lively spring day and returned to the task waiting for me at kitchen table. I began by writing that besides being a wife and helpmate to our dad, our mother had four children and each child thought he or she was her favorite. I smiled.

My husband and I were blessed when our son and his wife named their first child, our granddaughter, Emma Grace. Emma is named after my mother and my daughter-in-law's maternal great-grandmother, Grace. Little Emma is a spunky, intelligent girl with a twinkle in her eye. Her charm and smile are wonderful reminders of my mom and I am grateful for my precious memories that are always nearby, especially when I'm holding or interacting with Emma Grace.

May the Lord bless you from Zion all the days of your life; may you see the prosperity of Jerusalem, and may you live to see your children's children. (Psalms 128:5–6)

Amen!

Action Plan

1. Recall times that someone showed grace and love to you. It is not hard to remember a time when someone treated you better than you deserved. That person reflected God's grace and love to you. That person gave you a sense of being dearly loved.

2. Reflect on your parents and/or your important role models. If you can, thank them and share your favorite memories of them.

3. Ask yourself if you have any childhood "garbage" that needs to be forgiven. Remember, parents are not perfect. If you have made some parenting errors and feel estranged from your children, pray for encouragement to begin the healing process.

What's Your Mission?

For we are God's workmanship created in Jesus Christ to do good works, which God prepared in advance for us to do. (Ephesians 2:10)

Sara's mission statement: As a child of God it is my mission to love others honestly, believe God's promises, and rejoice in His presence!

Ephesians 2:10 states that as Christian women, we are God's prized possessions and He blesses each of us with unique talents and gifts. Our skills, interests, abilities, and backgrounds all vary. Paul, who is the author of Ephesians, emphasizes that by God's design our differences provide strength to the entire church and our lives become equipped for our personal journey. Throughout the Bible, God used imperfect men and women in extraordinary ways to further His earthly kingdom and transformed women of little or no faith into devoted servants.

In my writing class, the instructor suggested we all develop a personal mission statement to give our lives focus and balance.

Frankly, I thought it was a bit nerdy. Excuses flooded my mind: *nope...won't...don't have time...too busy...too lazy...too much thinking...* However, after that class I began to see mission statements everywhere. I saw mission statements clearly posted as I entered stores, strategically placed in doctors' offices, printed on church bulletins, and placed prominently on professional letterhead. Everywhere I went mission statements greeted me! Each business's statement was a unique written proclamation of core values and qualities they strived to incorporate into their companies. I received the message loud and clear: I needed to write my mission statement.

The process was challenging, but the product became a tool for measuring what I believe is important. I use my mission statement daily. I repeat it mentally every morning and think about it as I go to sleep at night. I keep it central to making decisions and if I am asked to commit my time and talent to a project, I check the opportunity with my statement. If it advances any one of my core values of love, belief, and joy, I am more likely to commit to the situation. I have also discovered that there are times when I have had to apologize or come to God and ask for forgiveness for my personal behavior and attitudes that have not been loving or joyful. My statement is a tool to keep me honest.

Creating a personal mission statement, one that really reflects your life principles, is not an easy task. More than anything, I wanted my statement to be a reflection of who I am in Christ: I am a sinner saved by grace. I wanted my philosophy to be in line with my Heavenly Father and I needed to bring the Holy Spirit into the process, so I prayed for guidance.

What would Jesus' mission statement look like, I wondered? What would he write in a few words? I started to search the Bible, and I think John 10:10 is perfect: "Jesus said, 'I have come that they might have life and that they may have it to the full.'"When we pair the Scripture from Ephesians 2:10 with John 10:10, we can see clearly that God's desire is for us to reach our full potential—to be the person He created us to become. God's intention is for our lives to be fulfilling and healthy emotionally, physically, and spiritually!

According to Stephen R. Covey in his book, *The 7 Habits of Highly Effective People*, writing a mission statement can be the most important activity an individual can undertake. He states that a mission statement is not something that you do overnight. It takes deep introspection, careful analysis, thoughtful expression, and often many rewrites to produce the final form. It may take you several weeks or even months before you are really comfortable with your mission statement and feel it is a complete and concise expression of your innermost values and directions. Stephen Covey suggests an annual review to make minor changes as additional insights occur or circumstances change.

My intent was to have a visionary statement, one broad enough to capture all facets of life and remain relevant in times of blessings and periods of adversity, a statement constructed with the flexibility to guide me in my day-to-day decision-making. Most importantly, I wanted my mission statement to reflect the kind of character I wanted to develop with God's help. And it needed to be simple so I could remember it! The process I used didn't take weeks or months. Within several days of persistence and contemplation the process unfolded naturally.

Beginning my mission statement, I reasoned that most adults can remember three facts, three items in a list, three things that need to be done; plus, there are three parts to the Trinity. I chose to use the number three during the creative process of defining my personal statement.

Then, I decided to incorporate a passage from a Scripture verse that really speaks to me. I used part of 1 John 3:1-2: "How great is the love the father has lavished on us that we should be called children of God. And that is what we are!" My statement would begin with, "As a child of God my mission is to..."

Next, I reflected on my core values. I brainstormed action words that resonated with my most basic beliefs, and narrowed them down to three verbs that represent what I find most valuable in myself and others. I decided on *love*, *believe* and *rejoice*. It was important for me to keep centered on Jesus Christ and his love. I needed to have my mission statement aligned with Scripture. I also decided to confirm that each word was truthful and precise, not grandiose or pretentious.

The final step was to expand these three foundational words into a phrase. I challenged myself to limit each phrase to a total of three words. I started with "Love" and added "others honestly." I realize that I can be judgmental and have repented many times for making a quick assessment of someone, and I have gossiped and found myself guilty of not being loving. I researched "love" in Scripture.

John 14:23 states that "Jesus replied, 'If anyone loves me, he will obey my teaching. My Father will love him, and we will come to him and make our home with him.'"*Love* is good! Now my statement read:"As a child of God my mission is to LOVE others honestly."

My next verb was *believe.* Because God is the solid rock on which I desired to build my life, believing His promises is crucial. I have struggled with my need for others' approval for personal validation. Subsequently, I wanted to remind myself to rely on God's love and approval, so my next three-word phrase became: "Believe God's promises." I checked with Scripture. John 20:27 affirmed "believe": "Then he said to Thomas, 'Put your finger here; see my hands. Reach out your hand and put it into my side. Stop doubting and believe.'" *Believe* is good! My statement expanded to: "As a child of God my mission is to love others honestly, BELIEVE God's promises..."

My final action verb was *rejoice. Rejoice* is such a happy word and I definitely want to be cheerful in all that I do. Being safe under my Savior's protection is a delight. I don't want to be afraid. I want to dance with joy, walk with enthusiasm, and live with confidence. My final phrase became: "Rejoice in His presence." But I had to check with Scripture first. Philippians 4:4 states, "Rejoice in the Lord always. I will say it again: Rejoice!" *Rejoice* is good! My personal mission statement was finished! As a child of God it is my mission to love others honestly, believe God's promises, and REJOICE in His presence.

Because I wrote and memorized my mission statement, I possessed one more go-to tool. I became aware of the times when

God arranged events in my life and times when I simply needed to rest in His presence. I began to mentally repeat my statement when placed in an uncomfortable situation or when I had a disagreement with someone. I possessed an instrument to combat the saboteur, the inner voice of self-deflating slander, who lurked in the dark shadows of my mind to hold me back and keep me from fulfilling God's purpose for my life.

Through the process of creating my mission statement I understood how God used a few simple words to help me clarify my belief in Him and my role as His child. I did not need a lengthy dissertation. My mission statement helped me stay aligned with God's purpose for me and I was able to view myself as He perceives me, as a worker in His kingdom. My heart was encouraged when I observed my personal growth. I know that I am more relaxed and attentive to my actions that reflect love, joy and belief. I find I am able to remove myself one level emotionally and think about a usually tense environment or circumstance more thoughtfully and less reactively. I am less rash when making decisions and base more of my evaluations on who I am as a child of God instead of what I think would please someone else. I am happier and more consistent.

A personal mission statement is a powerful internal statement of who you are and what you find important in life. Holding options up to your mission statement is a simple method for clarifying choices and defining personal boundaries. For example, if you find yourself in an ethical dilemma, referring to your mission statement can produce calmness. When asked to make a decision or give an opinion, mentally repeating your statement can help you instantly clarify actions and their consequences. It also gives you the freedom to react with wisdom and composure because you remain cool and maintain control of your emotions more easily.

What is your personal mission statement? If you don't already have one, remember that the Lord is good and He will refresh you with creative thoughts as you write. As you begin this adventurous process of reflection, contemplation, and becoming engaged in defining your core values and beliefs, rely on your own spirit to personalize it and make it yours!

I will instruct you and teach you in the way you should go; I will counsel you and watch over you. (Psalms 32:8)

Amen!

What's Your Mission?

Step One: Here are some prompts to get you started. Choose one or create your own. Remember to trust the process!

As a child of God it is my mission to:

My mission in life is to:

As a saved and redeemed sinner it is my mission to:

My mission as God's unique creation is to:

Step Two: Pick three words that reflect your core beliefs. (Prayer, a pencil, notebook, and a thesaurus are essential tools for this portion.)

Step Three: Add additional words to create three separate phrases. Limit the number of words in your phrases so it will be easier to remember (e.g., "Love others honestly"). Write your first draft.

Step Four: Put your first attempt away and let it rest for a day or two. Then, revisit and rewrite until it is just right for you. Soon your final statement will become a part of who you are in Christ!

Step Five: Post your mission statement where you will see it daily. Use the bathroom mirror, the dashboard of your car, or glue it into your daily planner and write it boldly on your monthly calendar. Use your senses and your preferred learning style to make your mission statement part of you! The more you see it, say it, and hear it, the deeper it will infiltrate your whole being!

Thrift Store Christmas Treasure

And God is able to make all grace abound to you, so that in all things at all times, having all that you need, you will abound in every good work. (2Corinthians 9:8)

O n our way to writing class, I shared with my commuting friends my desire to hone my public-speaking skills. The old adage, "Be careful what you wish for because you might receive it!" proved to be true, because within days I was asked to be the speaker for a Christmas tea. Without thinking about the consequences or the work involved, I agreed to be the guest speaker for this special holiday occasion for women residents of an assisted living facility/ rehab center or the attached nursing home. Age, education, mental alertness, physical disability, and other health concerns were different for each woman and the only common denominator was their need for care. I was nervous and frustrated that the event was within days and my search for an interesting and entertaining program topic evaded me. I was beginning to panic, so I decided to pray about my situation and ask God for help.

At the conclusion of my teaching day the following afternoon, I was on my usual route home and the traffic light turned red. As I impatiently waited for the green light to appear, I sensed a gentle nudge to interrupt my routine with a visit to the local thrift store. Something of significance commonly happens to me when I obey this inner signal, so I have learned to comply. I had driven past the store almost daily for twenty years and had never before felt inclined to stop. I wondered what treasure was waiting to be unearthed.

Once inside the clean and well-polished store, I noticed the racks of clothing were sorted by color instead of by size. One section of the store contained used wedding dresses and all the adornments needed to complete an entire wedding party. Except for the checkout clerk and the workers processing product in the back, I was the lone person roaming the store.

I wandered through the main level of the secondhand store, threading my way through racks of used clothing, shelves of shoes, walls of handbags, and a section of toys. Nothing significant popped out at me. I climbed the stairs to the second level and ambled through the assortment of bikes, computers, appliances, beds, couches and chairs, children's furniture, and a barrel full of mismatched golf clubs. Not finding a prized possession, I left the second level empty-handed, disappointed, and ready to abandon my pursuit of uncovering a prize.

Returning to the main floor, I edged my way through the aisles of housewares items. As I approached the exit, I spied a case filled with an assortment of glassware. Suddenly I knew that I had indeed discovered my treasure. Two cups stood next to each other on the first shelf and they appeared to be in perfect condition. I asked to have them taken out of the display, and on closer inspection verified that they were flawless. I estimated that the oversized white mug could contain sixteen or more ounces of coffee or cocoa and the delicately hand-painted miniature china teacup with its matching saucer could hold about four ounces of tea. They were opposites, and because of this I sensed that my treasure hunt was complete.

Inspiration for my Christmas tea presentation had not been on my shopping list, but that's what I received. I paid the marked price and was ecstatic that God had answered my prayer so quickly— within twenty-four hours! Pleased with my purchase and grateful to have obeyed the inner prompting, I drove home ready to write my holiday message.

My Christmas tea message would be rooted in Psalms 17:8: "Keep me as the apple of your eye; hide me in the shadow of your wings." It would be a resounding affirmation to each woman present that she was loved, cherished, and valued. I needed to convey the message that God's love and compassion for them was real and vibrant. I did not want them to think that they had been forgotten or placed into the discard pile like the cups that ended up in the thrift store. Because the two cups varied so much in their composition, I wanted to highlight the importance of accepting differences in each other and rejoicing in our similarities. I wanted my audience, many of whom carried heavy health burdens, to be renewed with hope and feel encompassed by God's love.

The evening arrived, and Christmas carols were sung, special cookies, hot tea, and coffee were enjoyed. The wonderful display of various homemade cookies, bars, and candy would usually appeal to me, but I found myself unable to enjoy one tasty morsel. When I tried to swallow a bite, it got caught in my throat and I had to cough. My mouth was dry and I feared I would make a spectacle by choking on the food and passing out, and that an ambulance would need to be called. The time for my talk arrived and I walked toward the podium with shaking legs and a fluttering heart. I placed a beautifully wrapped box containing the two cups on the podium, hoping this visual aid would rapidly engage my audience and keep their interest as well as buy me some time to gain composure.

I began my talk by paraphrasing from the book *Taste and See: Savoring the Supremacy of God in All of Life* by John Piper. The author states that as children of God and believers in Jesus Christ we have two major responsibilities: to have a grateful attitude and to love others. I explained that even though our circumstances may be difficult, having a grateful heart is the mark of a secure, healthy, and mature person. We know that our strength to be appreciative toward others comes from God and not ourselves. I shared that demonstrating a grateful heart may be as simple as using someone's name and specifically stating what action was appreciated. Even a smile or an acknowledgement of someone you meet in the hallway or at lunch is a good way of showing gratitude. We care about others because God cared about us. I went on to say that no two people are identical and there will never be another *you!* God designed each of us the way we are: with multiple strengths and also some weaknesses.

My message's main point was that although we are diverse, we have more in common to join us together than differences that divide us. I shared the information that the basic needs of love and acceptance, belonging, fun, a sense of competency, and the freedom to make choices are universal. The two cups wrapped inside the present would demonstrate the point that as dissimilar as they were, their purpose was the same.

I highlighted the fact that God's intent to create each of us as unique and special individuals is meant to be a blessing, but there are times when our differences seem so severe that the blessings are hidden. Sometimes we feel like an ordinary coffee mug and don't appreciate our worth. The coffee mug holds a lot of liquid or "burden." Its purpose is utilitarian and it gets used every day. I gave examples of the times a coffee mug may be taken for granted and not treated well, forgotten and placed on a garage shelf, or lost in the trash in the backseat of a car. A china teacup, on the other hand, is perceived as delicate and unable to bear the brunt of burdens. It may be kept out of use and placed on a special shelf because it is so fine. However, china glassware has been tested by firing it at a high temperature, proving its strength is merely hidden in its beauty.

It is very easy to compare ourselves to others who we believe are more valuable, the "teacups" in our lives. When we don't appreciate our distinct personalities and talents, we are unable to set healthy boundaries and can become wounded. I mentioned that there will be times when we all become delicate and fragile, requiring a little extra care and love. Perhaps we may even need to be placed in a safe and gentle environment to mend and become strong. There might be circumstances in our lives when we need to exchange the role of being a caregiver and become a gracious receiver, the latter being a situation that is unnatural for most women.

I reminded the women that God watches over each of His children and offers a loving and supportive heart, especially in times when we feel awkward, incompetent, and are hurting physically or emotionally. God shows us His daily presence in a variety of ways. It may be the kindness of a gentle word or a smile or a hug given unexpectedly. God's presence may be sensed through the loving attention of children and grandchildren, the beauty of nature and art, or the gift of music and wonderful food. Most important of all is the recognition of the simple message of God's love delivered through a birth in a manger.

At the conclusion of my talk, I removed the gift-wrapping from the box and shared my thrift store treasure hunt and how it inspired my message. I displayed the two cups and suggested that at this precious time of year we needed to remind ourselves that all of humanity is equal. It doesn't matter if we are mugs or teacups, common shepherds, angelic beings, or wise men from the East, we celebrate and rejoice in being loved and cared for by a Heavenly Father who will fulfill all our needs and keep us safe in the shadow of His wing.

Be joyful always; pray continually; give thanks in all circumstances, for this is God's will for you in Christ Jesus. (1 Thessalonians 5:16–18)

Amen!

Action Plan

God's love is a message everyone needs to hear. The knowledge that you are the apple of His eye may require an action on your part. What is God asking of you? Here are four questions to begin your self-examination.

1. How can God use my talents?
2. Who has God placed in my life to help me?
3. What is my first step in becoming obedient?
4. What thrift store treasure might represent me?

Jewels in Grandma's Crown

Children's children are a crown to the aged, and parents are the pride of their children. (Proverbs 17:6)

"**M**om, we are heading to Rochester. My water just broke! I just took a shower and everything is fine!" My daughter spoke excitedly yet calmly as she entered our bedroom in the early morning hours that Sunday.

I saw her expectant silhouette at the end of our bed and understood immediately that today my daughter and son-in-law's nine-month wait would come to an end. It was one o'clock in the morning and their home and hospital in Rochester was two hours away. "Will they make it to the hospital in time?" I asked myself.

I followed Bridget out of our room and into the kitchen, where I saw Chad standing, calm and self-assured, surrounded by their luggage. He smiled pleasantly and appeared confident that everything was under control. He gave me a thumbs up and left to load their car.

It was a strange feeling to stand idly in the hallway and view my daughter's confidence as she entered the first stages of the birthing process. I, on the other hand, felt helpless. I was concerned about their long drive to the hospital, and it must have shown on my face and body. My daughter hugged me reassuringly and said, "Mom, everything will be just fine. We called the hospital and the nurse told us we have plenty of time."

Those parting words did not ease my mind, and my memory of becoming her mother flooded into my thoughts. Bridget had been born within two hours of my water breaking, and she had also been ten days early. I whispered a silent prayer and gave them both a hug, then watched helplessly as the car lights disappeared down the driveway.

I shuffled back to bed and prayed for the safety of this young couple and God's intervening hand in all that was yet to come. I must have been at peace, because I woke up several hours later and noticed that had I missed the message Chad left at three o'clock a.m. His excitement was evident. They had indeed arrived home safely and called the hospital. They were advised to time her contractions and he added that Bridget was on her way into their bathroom for another shower.

"Take a shower again?" I thought." Just get to the hospital!"

There was no communication for several hours. The phone rang at six o'clock a.m. and Chad stated they were leaving for the hospital. I was surprised because I thought they would have been there a long time ago. Within a short period of time, Chad called yet again to tell us they had met with their midwife who told them, "You are definitely going to have this baby today. It could be four, six, or nine o'clock, but there will be a baby born today!" Chad said he would keep us informed about the birth of our first grandchild.

The wait consumed my day and I mentally replayed the morning's schedule: they left our home at one a.m., at three a.m. they arrived in Rochester, and at seven a.m. Bridget was in the labor and delivery room. I attempted to read the local newspaper, but my eyes kept drifting to the phone. I set up the ironing board and ironed clothes, but I still watched the phone. I wiped off the kitchen cabinets and scrubbed the floor, but I kept an eye on the phone. I vacuumed the living room furniture and remained inside all day. I was determined to not miss the next call. I made lunch and did a crossword puzzle, but none of these activities diverted my focus from moving the hands of the clock and generating a phone call—all to no avail. What was happening? Was there a medical emergency? Minutes and hours ticked by and finally, at 2:30 p.m. I called Chad's cell phone and left a message for him to call us as soon as possible.

Within minutes of leaving that message, the phone rang and Chad's pleasant voice said, "Hello, Grandma, Bridget gave birth to our baby at 2:33 p.m. and she wants to talk to you."

"Is it a boy or a girl? Is everything all right?" I asked.

Chad answered, "Everything is fine, and here is your daughter!"

"Mom, you and Dad have a grandson! Alexander Ryan is beautiful and everything went well and I feel great!" My daughter's voice was strong and full of pride.

I called the new grandpa, my husband, and within an hour we were on our way to the hospital, anxious to hold and love our newest family member. We were almost there when our cell phone rang and our daughter asked, "Where are you?" I thought it was humorous and perfectly fair that they were eagerly waiting for us to arrive.

Frank replied, "We're here, right by the hospital. We'll park the car and be there."

Bridget gave us clear instructions to her room, but we didn't have anything in the car to write on and we were naïve about navigating Mayo Clinic. We entered the hospital and found ourselves in a maze of corridors, tunnels, buildings, and doorways—most of them locked or closed. The unfamiliar network of passageways baffled even my husband, who has a great sense of direction. We stumbled upon an elevator and we arrived at the third floor, but once the doors opened we were confronted with more decisions, additional corridors, and more dead-ends. We returned to the elevators and went in the opposite direction, frustrated that we were so close. My patience was at its end. I was ready to cry!

Finally, wandering down another hallway, we noticed a sign with an arrow: "Obstetrics—straight ahead." We pushed the double doors open and entered into an area marked "Restricted." We felt it was a good sign when we heard a baby's cry. Clearly we were finally getting closer to our target! We followed the sound to the nurse's station and gave our daughter's last name. The station nurse searched the database and directed us down the hall.

The door to their room was partially closed, but I could hear my daughter's voice. We entered quietly and I saw my five-hour-old grandson, Alexander Ryan, wearing a blue knit cap, snuggled cozily in his proud daddy's arms. Our daughter looked fantastic. She appeared rested, proud, and glowed with love. Tears filled my eyes as I beheld the precious scene.

I will never forget the magnificent feeling of holding Baby Alex in my arms. I touched his unblemished, velvety-smooth face gently with my fingers. His body weight of seven pounds and six ounces felt wonderful in my arms. I sat on the bed by my daughter, unbundled his swaddled receiving blankets, and examined his perfectly formed nineteen-inch body. His strong legs kicked at the temperature change. His left eye squinted open, but closed quickly, unaccustomed to the bright light. He moved his little tongue and slept peacefully. I kissed his head and welcomed him into my heart. Grandpa was thrilled to hold Baby Alex, and his heart was captured too. We felt pride and thankfulness for the delivery of a healthy grandchild. It was love at first sight!

Both Frank and I were fortunate to have grandparents in close proximity as we grew up. My grandparents lived down the street and I visited them frequently. My grandmother came to my tea parties and ate sliced apples, cheese, and specially brewed tap water with me. Frank's grandmother made the best sugar cookies and crab apple pickles that he still remembers fondly.

We are thrilled to have four grandchildren now and our family will grow once more with a new baby's arrival soon. Our children and grandchildren do not live near us, but because our relationships with our grandparents were so valuable to us, we in turn treasure our time with our grandchildren. In between our monthly visits, we talk with each of our grandchildren on the phone frequently. Although those calls may not be lengthy, they are bonding and fun.

We try to attend their special sporting events, church and school functions, and of course, birthday parties. When the children come to our home, my husband takes the boys into his woodshop to create an object with them that they can take home. He gives them lawn mower, snowmobile, and four-wheeler rides and concocts silly ways to enjoy the outdoors. We play board games and card games, and sometimes I will play the piano while they sit on the bench and pound away with me, or they may sing and dance. I also love to read bedtime stories and retell stories about their parents when they were little. They are often left wondering if the tales are true. With my stash of art materials, we color, create projects, and make a mess. Although our home is in disarray by the time they leave, it is a lovely disorder. As I tidy up, I happily relive our time together.

There are no sweeter words than *Grandma* and *Grandpa*. God has been faithful and blessed us with the gift of being involved and loving grandparents. Being a grandparent is a reminder of God's great love for His children. A grandchild is a jewel in the crown of a grandparent—a diamond to be cherished and treasured!

If you, then, though you are evil, know how to give good gifts to your children, how much more will your Father in heaven give good gifts to those who ask him! (Matthew 7:11)

But Jesus called the children to him and said, "Let the little children come to me, and do not hinder them, for the kingdom of God belongs to such as these." (Luke 18:16)

Amen!

Action Plan

1. If you are a grandparent, intentionally develop a relation-ship and spend the time necessary to bond with your grandchildren. Children of all ages spell *love* T-I-M-E! For example: a friend of mine creates "date nights (or days)" with each of her grandchildren and spends time with them individually in addition to family time. Another friend keeps a notebook of all the funny things her grand-children have said. When they visit, one of the first things they ask about is her "special notebook" and if she has new entries. She has also taken pictures and written a simple book for each of her grandchildren, which I am sure will be cherished memories.

2. If you are not a grandparent, discover ways to relate to children. The infectious simplicity that is unique to chil-dren is invigorating. All children need love and accep-tance, and within your community there are children in need. Investigate your local options for encouraging and promoting a healthy environment for all children.

3. Give financial gifts to charities that assist children. Children's Charities of America supplies a list of the top children's charities at www.childrenscharities.org.

Looking Beyond the Mirror

Charm can mislead and beauty soon fades. The woman to be admired and praised is the woman who lives in the Fear-of-GOD. (Proverbs 31:30 MSG)

I was reading bedtime stories to my grandchildren, six-year old Alexander and birthday-boy Nicholas. Nicholas was still fired up and enjoying the limelight from his celebration of being *three*, not two. He was not ready for sleep! As I attempted to read and bring quiet and calmness into his world, he looked at me in the glow of the dim nightlight and asked, "Grandma, what are all those crosses on your face?" I answered with a question. "What crosses, Nick?" His little finger gently touched my forehead and he affectionately stated, "These Grandma, the crosses right here!"

That evening as I prepared for bed I removed my makeup, brushed and flossed my teeth, and closely examined my face in the mirror. I even retrieved a magnifying mirror from my makeup case to check out those crosses that Nick observed. I knew he saw the crinkles by my eyes, my smile and laugh lines, the damage from sun, and the evidence of age. As I applied moisturizer I thought to myself, "When did all those crosses appear?"

My husband and I vacation in Florida during two of Minnesota's winter months and our vacation spot is full of advertisements encouraging clients to schedule two-for-one laser or injection treatments for wrinkles. The models in the magazines and on the highway billboards are active middle-aged men and women. The not-so-subtle message is that you too could be as attractive and charming as the images and all that is needed is a visit to the clinic. The ads are tempting and appealing, but as wonderful as looking young and radiant may be, I know that it is more important to be beautiful and "wrinklefree" on the inside.

My mother is a perfect example of a woman who had the fear of God, and became more beautiful as she aged. Her trust in her Heavenly Father began when she was a child and increased throughout her lifetime. Her love for Jesus shined, and her inner beauty bubbled into her smile, her twinkling eyes, and her gentle ways. Her life's mission was to put Jesus first, others second, and herself last. Freely giving her time to help others, she became a witness of her faith through her actions. When my grandparents became fragile, my mother cared for them in our home. When he became immobile, my father was able to stay home because my mother cared for him and monitored his health concerns. Her garden was lovely and she seldom used any kind of herbicide or fertilizer. My mother enjoyed her grandchildren and created a fort for them in the backyard. She played with them and taught my daughter how to sew on an old treadle sewing machine. When she visited my family, she cleaned, helped our young family catch up on laundry, and made the best meatball-and-gravy dinners. She was unpretentious in nature and powerful in her simplicity.

I witnessed strangers approach her and remark about her attractiveness and resemblance to Katharine Hepburn. I always found this odd, because I was embarrassed by her lack of style and self-conscious when I was with her and she wore stripes mixed with plaids. At the age of ninety she exhibited the beginning signs of dementia, but was still able to live at home in her small community for some time. My mother never missed a Sunday church service and one fall day she attended a service where the pastor, who usually wore a suit, was attired in a white robe with gold raiment. At the end of the service she shook his hand warmly and told him he was beautiful. When the pastor stopped by for a quick visit the next day, she delightedly detailed her experience of shaking hands with Jesus and remarked on his pleasant appearance. At my mother's funeral, the pastor lovingly and humorously told this story.

I have been blessed to have aunts who share my mother's godly fear of the Lord, and when I am in their presence I feel the serenity they exude. I understand that the sense of peace and love that creates their inner beauty cannot be inherited; instead, it is a characteristic to be sought in one's heart. Fear of the Lord is good and will yield the following:

Wisdom (Proverbs 9:10)

A satisfying life (Proverbs 19:23)

Knowledge (Proverbs 1:7)

Goodness (Psalms 31:19)

God loves kindness (Psalms 103:11)

The fountain of life (Proverbs 10:27)

Deliverance (Psalms 34:7)

Riches, honor, and life (Proverbs 22:4)

Delight to God (Psalms 147:11)

Avoidance of evil (Proverbs 16:6)

Salvation (Psalms 85:9)

I want all of the above. I also want to be a beautiful woman as I age, but I don't want my beauty to come from the work of scalpels and lasers. I want the love of Jesus, which is an inner beauty, to be the first thing people notice about me. Maybe people will even see beauty when they notice the crosses on my face.

One sleepless night I was in our loft reading. I put down my book and walked over to the window to pull the fresh night air deeply into my lungs. I knelt and placed my arms on the windowsill as I gazed at the dark sky aglow with stars. I silently reflected on my unique childhood experience, telling the story to myself just like I would tell a bedtime story to my grandsons.

A narrow landing at the top of the stairs was the perfect spot for the rarely used attic door. Framed by glossy, light-yellow painted woodwork, this door was the entrance to a mysterious world of treasures, overflow from a family of six. This forgotten room contained boxes filled with strange objects, cartons with contents spilling over, disorganized bags, and collectible items of questionable value, all-having no purpose other than to fuel an inquisitive mind. The eaves and support beams were exposed, and the only light available, other than sunshine from a small window looking south, was a bulb that could be switched on by pulling a string. The dim light gave the room even more magic. The scent of mothballs completed an aura that was exotic to a five-year-old mind. By opening the door, a little girl's world changed from ordinary to extraordinary, from dull to creative, and she came to think of this as a treasured place where she could let her imagination loose.

The gentle child was loved by her family. Her mother read Bible stories and prayed with her every night before bedtime. When the child lay down to sleep in her single bed, she would snuggle against the wall to allow Jesus enough room to be comfortable as he lay by her side. She believed in his presence and was fearful that she would roll over and squish him. Drowsily, she would lie still, not wanting to disturb this special bonding time with her friend, Jesus. Every morning, she awoke refreshed and without a care.

One partly cloudy afternoon the young girl entered the enchanting room through the small door. As usual, she rummaged through the various items, creating her own fantasy world. After emptying the contents of a trunk and checking the inventory to see if anything had been added or taken away, she carelessly threw the things back inside and closed the lid.

Next she scooted onto the lumpy mattress of a metal cot by the window. A large, worn, multicolored quilt bunched up on top of the mattress made this spot very nest-like. The child snuggled down and looked out the small window. Her little arms were a perfect fit for the windowsill. She rested her head on her arms and sighed deeply. The window overlooked her backyard and she skimmed the sight below: the trees around the property, her playhouse, and the rock gardens and vegetable gardens where her mother spent a lot of time. Above her in the azure sky were clouds of cotton. Gazing into the clouds, she thought about her wonderful friend, the creator of all she saw. She was so thankful that He loved her.

With the sun in the background, one cloud became more striking than the rest and caught her attention. As she watched the sky, the interior of that wispy cloud parted and a man appeared. She clearly saw his white gauzy undergarment overlaid with a soft blue tunic with pleats draping off his shoulders. Her eyes traced up the flowing garment to an exceedingly serene face. Light brown, gently waving hair with wisps of gold swept over his neck and grazed his shoulders. His eyes exuded warmth and love. His gentle smile warmed her heart. She blinked and squinted to try to take in every detail, but the image disappeared as suddenly as it had arrived. Minutes went by, then as quietly as she had entered the room, the girl left. She knew she had been privileged to catch a glimpse of something she did not then and probably would never understand. She tucked the memory away and kept it safe in a trunk in her own mental attic, never sharing it with anyone. Thoughts and questions about the image were cemented in her subconscious and became a precious and unexplainable part of her childhood memories.

As a small child I was blessed to see Jesus, the real diamond! It had been natural for me to make room in my bed so I wouldn't squash my friend, Jesus, as he lay by my side. The unassuming and simple nature of childhood beckons, but the truth is that I am not a child. I am a wife, a mother, and a wrinkly grandmother with "crosses" on her face. I desire an adult woman's fear of God.

Recently, I played the old hymn, "Trust and Obey," by J.H. Sammis, on my piano and those two words are the summation of what it means to me to be a woman of faith, a woman who has a fear of God in her spirit. "When we walk with the Lord in the light of His word, what a glory He sheds on our way! While we do His good will, He abides with us still, and with all who will trust and obey." The woman who walks with God has a sense of peace and composure that is very attractive. Her language is edifying and builds up rather than destroys. Her wisdom is well placed and timely. Her thoughts and actions are transparent to others. She is not devious and manipulative, and her desire to please her Heavenly Father is foremost in her heart.

Developing a fear of God is a process and will take a lifetime. We will never be complete until we take our last earthly breath and are united with our Heavenly Father. Daily battles will continue, but we have a secret weapon: prayer. The supernatural gifts of the Holy Spirit will give us more courage than we thought possible. The very first step is to come humbly before the Lord and give up the mask of self-control to God-control. It is by far the most difficult decision to make, but one that will affect an entire family. The decision to trust and obey will change us from the inside out, and the by products of peace, love, and joy will abound.

I may well be an old woman before my eyes sparkle and my smile flashes as my mother's did. But I am working on shining the love of Jesus and reflecting in the mirror a woman who basks in the love of her Savior, like the woman described in Proverbs 31:30.

My action plan evolved over months and years. I know the importance of being in Scripture because it reminds me daily of God's love for me. I have a wall hanging that keeps me on task, reminding me that, "If your day is hemmed in prayer it is less likely to unravel!" I recognize my need to tamp the wild negative self-messaging and replace it with positive language, and I remind myself of the beauty of possessing a servant's grateful heart.

Your beauty should not come from outward adornment, such as braided hair and the wearing of gold jewelry and fine clothes. Instead, it should be that of your inner self, the unfading beauty of a gentle and quiet spirit, which is of great worth in God's sight. (1 Peter 3: 3-4)

Amen!

Sara's Daily Action Plan

1. Read a minimum of one daily devotional.

2. Recognize internal dialogue and self-talk. If negative language is flourishing, immediately replace it with self-affirming language.

3. Practice being at peace by remembering to have a grateful heart. When a situation is unpleasant or an outcome is not the desired one, ask, "Could it have been worse?"

Beauty Action Plan

Develop your own beauty action plan. I suggest you begin with three simple things you will incorporate into your lifestyle. Here are a few suggestions:

- Find a Bible that can be read in one year.

- Peruse the daily devotion books on the market and purchase one. In addition you may want a journal to track your growth and answered prayers.

- Ask God to give you a Scripture verse and memorize it and claim it as your gift from your Heavenly Father.

- Visit several denominations of churches and join the church family that will encourage your spiritual growth.

- Share with a trusted friend your desire to grow spiritually and ask for prayer support and encouragement.

Remember that God created you as a unique and special person, and your action plan should reflect your talents, desires, skills and needs!

Hats, Scarves, Aprons & Beads
Where, O Where, Will God Lead?

Enlarge the place of your tent, stretch your tent curtains wide, do not hold back; lengthen your cords, strengthen your stakes. For you will spread out to the right and to the left; your descendants will dispossess nations and settle in desolate cities. Do not be afraid; you will not suffer shame. Do not fear disgrace; you will not be humiliated. (Isaiah 54:2–4)

I had received an invitation to return to our previous church, Spirit of Joy, in Buffalo, Minnesota, and be the main attraction and speaker at their annual fall women's retreat. I checked the request against my newly written personal mission statement, and the answer was a clear *yes*! I could show love, believe that God would supply all my needs, and rejoice in friendship. As a teacher, I knew my students internalized a new lesson when they taught it to someone else, so I decided that I would share my process of writing a personal mission statement. By instructing others, my mission statement would absorb deeper into my spirit.

I was excited! I love the process of creating and facilitating new learning for myself and others, and being surrounded by old friends would be the frosting on the cake. When I shared my teaching plan for the retreat with a dear friend, she patiently listened as I explained my idea. Her reaction was supportive, but then she asked, "What are you going to do for humor?" She added that the best retreats have a comical side to complement the serious side.

What could I do that would be entertaining, humorous, and funky? Immediately I thought of all the talents I didn't have. The "I can't" monster roared ferociously within me and reminded me of all the things I couldn't do. I couldn't play the piano well. I couldn't sing on key. I couldn't remember jokes. I had no history with comedy. "I can't. I can't. I can't," I told myself.

"Enough!" I silently shouted at this discouraging dialogue. "I can do this," I told myself. My right brain, the creative side, launched into action. The first thing that occurred to me is that I have an uncanny ability to produce a very Scandinavian brogue as naturally as if I had been born with it. On the rare occasions I shared this accent in the past, people usually laughed. It was shortly after that realization that I first transformed myself into Aunt Sally. I decided to name her Sally because that is a derivative of Sara. Her coziness was based on my aunts' warmth, and her odd unpredictability and exuberance was a surprise even to me. I wasn't sure how she would encourage her audience to participate in the silly and amusing activities I had planned, but I trusted Aunt Sally to be extremely convincing. I loved her instantly and she represented my outgoing, self-assured, and creative self. I knew she could do it.

Her vintage 1950s ensemble came from the closets of supportive friends and family. A favorite blue-and-white dress was a gift from the trunk of Frank's mom, and it was an instant match with how I pictured Aunt Sally. With the help of Frank's mom, Sally gained an apron trimmed with rickrack from an antique store, round vintage gold trifocals, large pearl earrings, pop beads, and a retro pink hat with a droopy flower. Aunt Sally's attire was topped off with nylons rolled down around the knees, a handkerchief placed up her sleeve, a pair of brown, laced shoes that had belonged to Frank's grandmother, and an "Uffda" pin. She was perfect! Her look evoked exactly what I desired—a spunky, vivacious woman with an attitude that let everyone know she was her own person. Watch out, world!

Now that I had the character, I needed humorous material. Just in time, the local paper printed the police report, which doubles as the local gossip section. It was rich with real-life humor. A 911 call from a lake resident asked for immediate police action to stop the irritating water-skiers who mooned them as they tried to enjoy their lakefront decks. Another police response was needed because a man dressed in a hospital gown was wandering downtown. He did not have any underwear on. A third call asked for police intervention simply because some kids were being too loud. I wove some of the true police incidents around a few "Ole and Lena" jokes and soon my character had the bits and pieces to create an entertaining and original skit. I was pleased and secure that I had the two parts needed: humor and substance! I practiced my Aunt Sally shtick on my husband and my daughter and her husband. My son-in-law thought it was hilarious. I was bolstered by their reaction!

My first Aunt Sally outing was the women's retreat. I was alone changing into my Aunt Sally outfit and I prayed for God's assistance as I rolled my nylons below my knees. I needed His strength to muster the courage to do this crazy routine. He supplied my need. Aunt Sally ambled out from her hiding place and surprised the women with her long-vowel-filled dialogue. I was energized by their reception and Aunt Sally's timing for her jokes was on target. I beamed with pride at what God and I had accomplished! If I could have physically done it, I would have jumped up and clicked my heels together as I exited.

Afterwards Aunt Sally chatted comfortably in the front of the room by the fireplace, but soon excused herself and returned to the bedroom. Within minutes, I appeared as my real self and I taught my mission statement process. The women present were bonded with each other through laughter and the rest of the afternoon fell into place easily. I left the retreat invigorated with a sense that God was at work and a new plan was developing.

Aunt Sally's next excursion was the following month in Seattle, Washington for my Uncle George's ninetieth birthday. Encouraged by Aunt Sally's success at her first outing, I called his son, my cousin, and offered to do my character for the party. He readily accepted. Uncle George was the cousins' favorite uncle and he enjoyed each of us as much as we cherished him. About twelve cousins and their spouses traveled from all over the United States to celebrate with him. Before I transformed myself once more into Aunt Sally, I asked God for reassurance that He was fully supportive. I was dressed as Aunt Sally, and as I entered the bathroom to add a zesty bit of blush to my cheeks, I felt overwhelmed with this dumb idea. I was inching close to abandoning the whole crazy notion when I sensed God whisper, "I created the Grand Canyon, don't you think I can help you with this?" I was confident after that message and Aunt Sally did the same routine she had done for the women's retreat, but was inspired to add more flair. Because Uncle George had lived for many years in Park Rapids, he identified with the local police report humor and that set a nice tone. I added more jokes and worked in some family humor, then led the group in singing "Happy Birthday." No one present had expected Aunt Sally, including my brothers. I shocked them with my character and one of my brothers couldn't believe *she* was Sara. I had a ball!

Aunt Sally's Ministry was dreamed up on the plane ride back to Minnesota. One of our cousins had brought some of my grandmother's hats and the girl cousins ended up picking out their favorites. That was just a coincidence, but it started me thinking, "What is going to happen to Aunt Sally now?" With her dress, hat, apron, beads, and handkerchief packed into my suitcase, I thought it would be a shame to not use her again. I relived the humor and good-natured relationship building and connections she accomplished. In just fifteen minutes, a lot of human barriers could be crossed and healthy friendships created.

I envisioned Aunt Sally's Ministry to incorporate the character of Aunt Sally with audience involvement. I spent an entire summer developing these activities and collecting antique accessories. I planned to divide the audience into groups and led lighthearted lessons to engage them and increase their learning through participation. The loveable and peculiar character, Aunt Sally, would begin the retreats with her gimmick, add group participation, and then I would come back as the real me and give an inspirational message about God's love. However, my need for approval was still important and since my mother had passed away, I couldn't receive her blessing. I needed affirmation. I called my Aunt Dylee, Aunt Glady, and Uncle Helmer and asked for their prayerful support. They enthusiastically endorsed my vision and attended several presentations. I read Scripture and relied on 1 Thessalonians 5:24, "The one who calls you is faithful and he will do it." I knew that unless God was involved, Aunt Sally's Ministry would not flourish. As usual, Frank supported my new endeavor. My brother also encouraged me and offered some helpful business advice. I was off and running! I was excited and free to create outlandish, eccentric, and unique activities.

Aunt Sally's Ministry's first official presentation was in my hometown church, the place where I worshipped with my family as a child and was confirmed and married. Before my presentation, "Unwrapping God's Present for Today," I wrote in my journal as I waited in the bathroom for my entrance cue. I also read Isaiah 62:4 and I was reassured by the phrase, "for the LORD will take delight in you!"

Aunt Sally made a spectacular entrance, stomping loudly down the church stairs, flinging the door open and tripping into the room, and surprising her audience. Encouraged by her comedic flair, jokes, and gusto, the audience members readily chose costume pieces as part of the activities. Laughter is good medicine, and I was thankful to hear healthy giggles from women of all ages as they tried on the whimsical hats, aprons, and necklaces.

Sometimes in my presentations the women helped each other decide what colors coordinated with their clothes. In my search for vintage hats I fell in love with many of them, but I paid twelve dollars for a tan-and-brown hat that was very elegant. It was always fun to see who chose that hat and I usually whispered to them that they had excellent taste. I received many donated aprons, some with delicate cross-stitch embroidery. Women who had saved their mothers' handkerchiefs brought them to me so that they could get good use during my programs. Soon I had a great supply of props and the audience was up swaying and singing to songs, joining in a chorale reading, or participating in a quiz. One woman even forgot that the handkerchief she held was a prop and blew her nose into it. Oh well, that's show biz.

Just like a diamond is cut to show off its brilliance, by stepping outside my comfort zone I uncovered a previously hidden element of my personality. Aunt Sally became an extension of me. I was not constrained or limited by lack of confidence. My well-intentioned character became an opportunity for me to revert back to a simpler time when children dressed up and role-played, when good-natured humor was popular, and hurtful sarcasm was not funny. I became Aunt Sally with vigor and embraced the edginess of doing something so out of character. I had never thought of myself as being particularly funny, but Aunt Sally allowed that part of my personality to shine.

One of my favorite presentations was my Mother's Day program. In this presentation I honored the beautiful memory of my mother, shared the gift of becoming a parent myself, and delivered the message of God's love for us as our Heavenly Parent. I had so much fun and I felt aligned to God's fulfilling purpose for my life. I think He was pleased!

At another Aunt Sally presentation I was approached to become a speaker for Stonecroft Ministries, a nondenominational and international ministry for women. Stonecroft organizations are located throughout the United States and as I prayed about the offer I became convinced that spreading the Good News was consistent with my mission statement and would advance the knowledge of God's love. I prepared a topical and interactive presentation entitled "Too Much or Not Enough: The Dilemma of Parenting with Balance." My Aunt Sally character was not included in these talks; however, her courage accompanied me wherever I went. I included my personal testimony, including the story of my failing grade in health class. I told how becoming a child of God had changed my life. My husband was supportive and together we traveled throughout the Midwest. Being a speaker for Stonecroft Ministries was a journey of faith. I asked for God's truth to be told as I represented myself as a woman who recognized her Savior loved her so much. I was busy and happy. I felt fulfilled and valued. I loved the creativity of developing and delivering these lessons, and it blended well with my mission to tell my faith story. Frank was content, the kids were occupied with their lives, I was a new grandmother and a hospice volunteer, and was busy creating new friendships. Life was a treat. Life was good!

Aunt Sally opened the door to other opportunities. I had donated a computer to a program in our county that supports adult women returning to school and when I dropped it off, I entered into a conversation with the new Community Education Director. A woman overheard us talking and said, "I know you. You did that Aunt Sally thing at Blueberry Pines. You were so funny!" I soon learned from her that there was an opening for the Parents Forever Coordinator position and I was offered the job. Parents Forever is a University of Minnesota curriculum for divorced parents who have children under the age of eighteen. Emphasis in class is placed on what is best for the children and includes suggestions on how divorcing parents can alleviate trauma for their children. I accepted, and facilitated a fact-based eight-hour training session.

Through decades of teaching, parenting two children, nurturing four grandchildren, sustaining a marriage of many years, and the subsequent desire to have a meaningful retirement, I have loved being unique and creative. I rely on God for inspiration. In the creation of my loveable and whimsical character, Aunt Sally, His input was more important than finding hats, beads, aprons, or handkerchiefs! As I reflect, I realize that my path has often involved creative thinking as a tool to adapt and survive the changes around me. My creativity also allows me to find ways to get past my own insecurities in order to do positive things and discover more facets of myself. I am really quite shy and reserved, but Aunt Sally with her boisterous attitude and outlandish activities propelled me into a new light, illuminating previously unseen talents and abilities.

I have chosen the way of truth; I have set my heart on your laws. I hold fast to your statutes, O Lord; do not let me be put to shame. I run in the path of your commands, for you have set my heart free. (Psalms 119:30–32)

Amen!

God Will Lead Action Plan

God needs you to believe in your brilliant, diamond-like qualities. He wants to polish your talents and gifts so you will shine, and He needs you to be a worker in the kingdom. There is so much to do and the workers are few. Believe in God's power and don't get caught up in the destructive growls of the "I can't" monster! You are a unique and special person and our Heavenly Father delights in you! Know this in your heart!

1. Begin to put faith into action. Set aside time to be in nature or listen to music and talk to your Lord. Sit and be with Him and let the Holy Spirit minister to your heart, and soon new ideas and thoughts will flow. Write down the ones that build on your strengths and pray that God will confirm the direction He desires you to take. Clarity will come!

2. Read Scripture to encourage your journey. Start with Romans 8, and read it out loud many times. Hearing, seeing, and saying Scripture encourages and cements new insights. Mark your favorite Bible verses and refer to them whenever negative self-talk appears.

3. In your talks with God, share your concerns and cares. He knows all about them already, but He loves to spend time with you! Anticipate a response to your requests and be alert that God's ways are usually exciting, challenging, and invigorating! He won't do the work for you, but He will empower you to do His will.

How to Stay Out of the Trash: Relationship, Reliance, and Restoration

The boundary lines have fallen for me in pleasant places; surely I have a delightful inheritance. I will praise the Lord, who counsels me; even at night my heart instructs me. I have set the Lord always before me. Because he is at my right hand, I will not be shaken. Therefore my heart is glad and my tongue rejoices and my body also will rest secure. (Psalms 16:6–9)

We were going to our daughter's home for a visit and in anticipation of our arrival she told Alex, our six-year-old grandson, that we were coming. He was excited and made one offhand comment, which when relayed to me, brought tears, "That Grandma Sara has a lot of Jesus in her heart!" It could be because he had just been at our home and I asked him to be careful around Grandma's workspace—I did have my Bibles and papers stacked in a pile—or it was simply because he recognized something in my spirit and connected with it. I don't know, but I felt blessed. When we sat down to a lovely walleye dinner at their home the following night, we held hands to pray before the meal. Alex was asked if he would like to start the prayer, but he declined, so the offer was extended to three-year-old Nikko (Nicholas). He smiled and prayed his nighttime prayer, "Dear Jesus, thank you for loving me and keeping me safe!" He paused and looked at us with his huge blue eyes. His dad thanked him and then started our table grace, "Come Lord Jesus be our guest..." It was such a beautiful and tender moment. I love the openness and often-unintentional humor that occurs around those little ones.

Four tub-style chairs covered in yellow suede surround our dining room table. The table when extended will easily seat ten, but when we have a family meal there, I don't allow the kids to sit in the chairs. Alex asked how old he needed to be to sit in a gold chair and I answered, "When you are eleven." He thought for a moment and then proceeded to address Emma and Nikko. "I will be the first grandchild to sit at the table in the good chairs!"

God's desire is for us to be seated at His banquet table and have the knowledge that the good chairs are waiting for us. We don't earn our seat at the table like my grandchildren; we are already blessed to be children of God and our place setting is secure when we believe in Him. "Therefore, as we have opportunity, let us do good to all people, especially to those who belong to the family of believers," (Galatians 6:10).

There are three areas that are important to consider so that we're able to stay out of life's garbage can and remain at the banquet table where we are fed and nourished and our needs are supplied. First we must have a relationship with God, experiencing God in our lives and knowing who God is and how He works. I have been told that a relationship with God is like a dance. We must be closely involved with Him in order to know what our next step will be. I loved to dance the old-time waltz with Frank's dad, Ken. It is one of my favorite memories from the thirty-nine years he was my father-in-law. He made dancing easy and enjoyable. The motions of his hand on my back gave me clues as to how I should move. Ken was in control on the dance floor and I could easily follow. Because I allowed Ken to lead, we danced beautifully.

I was challenged during dark times to forfeit all ownership of self. Although I established a relationship with Jesus as my best friend, I am still learning to trust him and obey the quiet promptings and discern his will. I know he gives me cues just as my father-in-law's hand on my back told me how to move in our waltz. Every day, I require God's help in overcoming some self-defeating fear or behavior. On a daily basis, I am reminded to cede control of my life to God and His plan and purpose. I am dependent on Him to bring friendships and the fellowship of other believers into my life. I need His guidance to affirm and share God's love with others. I know that He sees the future and I trust Him to bring me into each new day with gratitude and thankfulness.

Reliance is another skill that needs to be considered. It begins with faith. I know that I have a Heavenly Father and I have been told over and over in multiple ways how much He loves me. I witness His love for me when I go for my daily walk. I am often brought to tears when I lift my head to observe His world around me. My reliance is reinforced through reading Scripture. Often my reading is only a one- or two-minute pondering over a morning devotional before the start of the day, but it reminds me that the best part of my day is yet to come, and keeps me focused on the path He has designed for me. Many times in the evening as I go to bed, I repeat my mission statement and evaluate where I fell short, but I also celebrate with God where I succeeded. No one else has my experiences, skills, DNA, hurts, scars, joys, talents, or weaknesses, and therefore I need to first and foremost rely on God and the Holy Spirit for guidance, patience, love, and acceptance. God is the only one I need to please. Being a pleaser and suppressing my true identity has been a struggle throughout my life, but with God's daily help, I am becoming truer to the person He designed me to be.

Restoration for me is being able to let go of my daily agenda and rest in the knowledge that God is my guide. It is the freedom to believe that Jesus is truly my best friend and I am empowered through the divinity of the Holy Spirit. It is being present in the moment and not projecting "what-ifs." Restoration is a place of safety for me. Sometimes I have looked in the rearview mirror to tell me where I have been. That isn't a bad thing, but it is easy to veer off into the ditch when my eyes aren't focused on the road ahead. Restoration means acknowledging the past but staying in the moment and looking toward the future with curiosity, obedience, and trust. I had the wonderful experience of being a child who received a lovely gift, but eventually I grew up and threw the gift away. God, with all the love in His heart, restored my childhood present just as he restored me.

Betty the Beautiful Bride stood regally on the shelf above the cash register in the small local grocery store. Every day that December when school was over, I detoured to Main Street on my way home and pressed my nose to the glass door to get a glimpse of this elegant doll. In all of my eleven years I had never seen a doll so beautiful and the reflections of the Christmas decorations and streetlights made her seem even more magical.

The full-length box that housed the bride doll was open to show off her dress and accessories. The dress was white taffeta with ruffles edged in sparkling silver. Her soft tulle veil was held in place with a crown of daisy-like flowers. Her round blue eyes were friendly, and her gentle smile encouraged a return grin of my own. She was complete with matching gloves, a beaded pearl choker, and glass slippers like Cinderella's. As Christmas Eve and winter vacation approached, Betty disappeared from the store shelf. I was disappointed that I would no longer be able to enjoy her.

Imagine my surprise as I unwrapped my present on Christmas Eve and beneath the paper was Betty the Beautiful Bride. I loved Betty and played with her every day. I carefully dressed and undressed her, and I was always conscientious with her accessories and never misplaced or lost an item. I wanted her to remain as perfect as she was on Christmas Eve.

When winter vacation ended, I carefully carried Betty to school in the original box. I was bursting with pride, expecting jealous "ooohs" and "aaahs." I carried her into my classroom and set her on the shelf by the window. From my desk I could look at her during the entire day. I was surprised when no one commented about Betty.

No one said, "What a lucky girl you are to have such a wonderful gift." No one paid much attention to Betty. No one else thought she was the most incredible doll in the world. She did not inspire the response I had imagined. No one cared about my doll. I carried her home with a heavy heart, but I still loved her immensely!

Years passed. Betty lost her veil, her shoes, her dress, her pearl choker, and her matching gloves. Betty also lost the little girl who loved her. My mother kept her around for years and eventually dressed her in a baby's blue jogging suit. My own children played with Betty, but she was not a gorgeous bride doll anymore. When we were cleaning out my childhood home after the death of my mother, I placed Betty into a black garbage bag and threw her away.

Forty-six years after I unwrapped Betty the Beautiful Bride, I was returning home from a visit up north and I stopped at a stoplight. I sensed that I needed to go into the antique store on the corner. I have learned to listen, so I parked my car and walked into the store. As I entered, I spotted an exact copy of Betty, box and all, above the cash register. She was surrounded by other old dolls, but none were as beautiful. I asked to see her more closely and as the manager lifted the box from the display, I could see that Betty was perfect except for two things: she was barefoot and her necklace was missing. She was an exact copy of the doll from my childhood. Without hesitation I paid the tag price. I left the store and placed Betty in the passenger seat of my car and she accompanied me to my home. Her blue eyes twinkled in the sunshine and her smile was as sweet and gentle as the first day I saw it. A small tangible piece of my childhood was restored, just as my simple childlike trust and whole-hearted faith had been restored.

A few more years passed and I retired from teaching. We moved and built a new home, and my doll in her box moved to Northern Minnesota with us. When Aunt Sally was newly birthed I felt insecure about teaching my mission statement process and I questioned if what I was thinking was accurate. Once more in my car, I was headed out of town and approaching another little antique store. I thought, "How cute, I think I will stop in there!" Standing in a crib to the right of the door was another Betty doll, half the size of mine. Her dress was a perfect replica, and she was complete with shoes and choker. How could this be? I looked at the price tag and was bowled over. I left the store without purchasing the second doll, but I couldn't stop thinking about her. I went home after my excursion and told my husband about the smaller Betty. He thought I was being a bit silly, and who needs two old bride dolls? But I continued to think about the doll. I went back a few days later and purchased her. God didn't just give me one doll—He gave me two!

I pondered why I had received these two special dolls. I was thrilled and surprised to have found even one Betty doll, but what was the lesson? I believe both dolls represent God's viewpoint that I am loved and have value beyond measure. God loved me so much that He would not leave me unattended, forgotten, and alone and gave me the gift of Jesus Christ. In addition, the first doll's message was an affirmation that I was on the right track. I could forge ahead into new territory and know that I was not on my own. God was holding my hand and providing all the confidence I needed. The second doll, smaller than the first Betty, appears to represent the newness of trust and obedience. I am still challenged to confront tendencies that defy the real me, but my future will not be a repeat of my past. Every morning I am excited to begin my day with Him and turn my multiple facets toward the light and slowly appreciate each diamond-like sparkle.

Arise, shine, for your light has come and the glory of the Lord rises upon you. See, darkness covers the earth and thick darkness is over the peoples, but the Lord rises upon you and his glory appears over you. (Isaiah 60:1–2)

Amen!

Action Plan

1. Journal about the following: How do relationship, reliance, and restoration apply in your life?

2. If you have been stuck looking through the rearview mirror too long, talk about your needs with a trusted friend, pastor, life coach, or professional counselor.

3. How can you actively keep yourself out of the garbage and begin to value your multiple facets?

Afterword

And the God of all grace, who called you to his eternal glory in Christ, after you have suffered a little while, will himself restore you and make you strong, firm, and steadfast. (1 Peter 5:10)

I t is early in the morning and the time has arrived to begin the end. In some ways this chapter is the most difficult to write because I realize a part of me is ending as well. I am completing a task I was instructed to begin years ago, although in retrospect I am not sure what I would have written. Initially, I thought *Diamonds in the Garbage* would be about the wonderful God-filled women in my life. I thought that I would interview and write about friends, family, and acquaintances. I would tell their stories and how they found strength in their weaknesses and courage to overcome obstacles and fulfill God's purpose in their lives.

I never thought that my life experiences would become the story. I didn't realize that God needed me to uncover my garbage can and dig into my trash to find the diamond—living with the knowledge of God's undying love for me! I didn't know the impact of being spanked and shut in a closet at the age of four would be part of the garbage. I didn't realize that my childhood vision of Jesus Christ would ever be stated, much less written about. I didn't know that my seventh-grade health class "failure" was so devastating and impacted my self-concept. I didn't know that symptoms of depression visited me on and off throughout my life. I didn't comprehend how deeply affected I was by the loss of my best friend to cancer. I didn't perceive that the imaginary rock attached to my leg and immobilizing me was *me*! I wasn't aware that my lack of trust in God caused me to use self-sufficiency to insulate me from honest and meaningful connections. I didn't fully grasp how much courage I would need to take one baby step into the unpredictable and unknown. I didn't fathom that I would need the new armor of trust as I became obedient.

There are two sayings from the 1970s that still ring true to me: "God Doesn't Make Junk!" and "You are thumb body special!" The former was a reminder that we are all created in His image and even on our worst days, we have worth. A thumbprint character with a happy face and little stick arms and legs accompanied the latter statement. The idea behind the "thumb body" was to encourage us and remind us that we are special. We all have unique fingerprints and DNA. Even siblings are born with a wide range of differences and can be opposites in personality, temperament, and talents. In the data bank of life we are exclusive, never to be repeated again. That is no accident. That is by God's design.

God delivers a love note every day in a multitude of ways. He sends a "You are thumb body special!" memo through the people in our lives, nature, our interests and hobbies, our dreams and hopes. God supplies His presence in the direst circumstances. He is in the business of restoration and is a master at renovation. He bends, polishes, and shines our spirits and wills into perfect harmony with His will. God doesn't do a little touch up. It is a complete refurbishment that starts on the inside, right in the center of your being, your heart. His desire is for us to be fully balanced and able to withstand the storms of life.

The process of healing and restoration of the broken parts of our lives begins when God, in the personhood of Jesus Christ and with the guidance of the Holy Spirit, is invited into our hearts. The garbage is loaded up and hauled away and the newly restored life becomes a brilliant multi-faceted diamond.

I recently located journals I wrote years ago and two entries were prominent. One was my personal experience with my daughter as we both of lit candles in a cathedral in downtown Oslo, Norway. I remembered praying as I lit the small white candle at the front of the sanctuary for my will to be aligned with God's will. I recalled silently thanking Him for my parents of Norwegian descent and for my mother's gift of faith. Inside this beautiful church, I quietly thanked God for all His gifts throughout the years and I felt blessed.

Another entry was written the day before my husband had bladder cancer surgery. This is what I wrote:

"Frank is scheduled for surgery tomorrow morning. God is guiding our lives and setting our path. Whom shall I fear and why should I be afraid? God is with us and his infinite mercy surrounds me and keeps my family safe. God knows the beleaguered sense within my heart. God is my friend, my deliverer and my source of strength. He will be with me today, tomorrow, and forever. I will have trust, faith and love beside me. I know that all is well and God is in control. Peace is at hand and death will have no sting. I am not afraid."

Through the writing process, I have learned a lot. Every day is a new day and a new challenge will certainly arise, but it is a gift to place all concerns into His hands. I understand that every day I am given a choice: either commit every minute detail to Christ, or try to handle some of life by myself and only bother God with the big stuff. I know which one God desires and I also know the consequences of self-sufficiency.

I want to be the butterfly smelling the flowers. I desire to be the strong, confident woman God intended me to be. I aspire to be a trusted worker in His kingdom and produce good fruit. I long to engage passionately within my God-given talents and live a fulfilling life.

I want the same for you, dear reader. I pray that you will be captured by your desires and begin the recharging process of getting out of the junk pile and becoming completely restored into God's loving and waiting arms. I pray that out of your garbage there will emerge a beautiful jewel—a diamond of exquisite quality, strength, and brilliance. Blessings, dear friend!

Therefore, if anyone is in Christ, he is a new creation; the old has gone, the new has come! (2 Corinthians 5:17)

Amen!

Action Plan

1. Acknowledge that you have fears and write them down.

2. Ask God to begin the process of restoration. Ask Him to show you what to do.

3. Faithfully meditate upon God's word and praise Him for what He is and what He will do in your life.

4. Expect to take one step at a time. God will direct your path and supply the resources you need at just the right time. Ask for the gift of faith as you enter into a new covenant with your Heavenly Father. Enjoy the friendship of Jesus Christ, and follow the direction and comfort of the Holy Spirit.

Suggested Scripture:

Psalms 27:1-3

Psalms 34:4-5

Psalms 55:4-8

Psalms 63: 1-8

Psalms 77:12

Psalms 91

9 781613 792131